THE
RADFORDS

THE RADFORDS

MAKING LIFE COUNT

Sue ♡ Noel

m
B
MIRROR BOOKS

We would like to dedicate this book to all of the people that have bought it and supported us on our journey but, most of all, we would like to dedicate it to all of our children and our parents.

MIRROR BOOKS

Written with Paddy Shennan.

1

First published in hardback in Great Britain and Ireland
in 2024 by Mirror Books, a Reach PLC business.

www.mirrorbooks.co.uk
@TheMirrorBooks

ISBN: 9781915306890
Hardback ISBN: 9781915306500
eBook ISBN: 9781915306517

Photographic acknowledgements:
The Radfords' personal collection.

Every effort has been made to trace copyright.
Any oversights will be rectified in future editions.

Editing and Production: Simon Monk, Christine Costello, Harri Aston

Printed and bound by CPI Group (UK) Ltd,
Croydon, CR0 4YY.

Contents

Introduction

Welcome to our crazy, wonderful world

We haven't just been addicted to love during our long and happy marriage – for most of it, we have also been addicted to having children. As addictions go, we think it was a pretty healthy one because it was motivated by nothing other than love – love for each other, and the love of having children.

We are Britain's biggest family, and proud of it.

This wasn't the plan, however. Indeed, looking at the size of our brood, you might think there was absolutely no family planning involved whatsoever!

How we actually came to have 22 kids – rather than the three we had originally been thinking about – is all explained in the following pages, along with so much else.

It could have all been so different, as there were times during our journey that we very nearly hit the end of the road – before, thankfully, other avenues opened up, and more children joined our ever–growing family.

A nightmare business decision threatened to tear our marriage apart when we were mum and dad to just seven children. We lost our way. We lost so much money. We could have lost our house – and could so very easily have lost each other.

Later, a much-regretted vasectomy could then so easily have left us with just nine children. We feared there was no way back – or, rather, no way forward, to having a bigger family. But sometimes, we found out, you have to "reverse" if you want to make progress! We could so easily have lost Tillie, our 14th child, when she was just 18 months old, but, thanks to a combination of fate and our wonderful National Health Service, she pulled through. Then we suffered the heartbreaking tragedy of losing darling Alfie, our 17th child, which left us devastated and in total despair. How could we possibly pick ourselves up and carry on after suffering such anguish? We really didn't think we could. Perhaps it was Alfie, our guardian angel, who showed us the way.

We know there have been so many little miracles along the way, and that we have so many blessings to count. Please believe us when we say we count them on a regular basis. We know how incredibly fortunate we are – and we give thanks for that every day. All we have to do is look at our children – along with our grandchildren (10 at the time of writing!) – to realise we are living the most extraordinarily happy lives.

Some might say the first "Radford miracle" began when we were a couple of ordinary teenagers who happened to be madly in love with each other. How many lovestruck kids are told "it won't last" by those who apparently know better? With us, they probably thought they were on extremely safe ground with their prediction of doom – especially when, with one of us still in school and the other still in college, we discovered our first child was on the way. Penniless, clueless and far too young to know much about anything, how on earth could we have possibly negotiated our way through such a seemingly calamitous and catastrophic situation? You're about to find out.

Our lives today, it goes without saying, are very different to when we were daft kids starting out as a couple who had each other – but not much else. Over the years, our family grew, we developed what is now a thriving bakery business, and then became the subjects of an increasingly popular TV series – which, in turn, helped us launch and grow a second successful business via the ever–expanding world of social media and its multiple platforms. We will explain, however, why we initially said a very definite "No, thank you" to the prospect of TV fame.

There are so many good things that have come from us appearing in the nation's living rooms on a regular basis – but, although they are thankfully outweighed by the positive, you will also be able to read about some of the negative and truly horrendous things we have been subjected to since agreeing to walk into the spotlight.

This book will take you on the rollercoaster ride we experienced to get to where we are today. We cannot quite believe it all happened – and maybe you won't be able to believe some of it, either! Those little miracles, we're glad to say, just kept on coming – and we are delighted to be able to celebrate them all in this first in-depth look at our lives.

For us, it's so lovely to be able to give you this larger-than-life story – in our own words. We know many of you may have seen us on TV, and you might think you know us quite well – but there are things we talk about in this book that have never been on TV. It's much more detailed, and goes far deeper into our lives.

Recalling the many different stages of our lives has been so fascinating. Obviously, some of our experiences have been terribly sad, but it's been nice to look back and think about when the kids were younger and what they were like at particular ages. We have such busy lives we don't often get the time to reflect, so this has been so nice and rewarding for us. We have loved reminiscing, and writing this book together has helped us realise what a great life we have had. We have learned so much during our amazing adventure together. For example, after having 11 boys and 11 girls, we will tell you which sex is by far the easiest to bring up! Our lives couldn't be more full – or fulfilling. And there is so much more to look forward to. We have no idea what some of that will be, but we know one thing – it won't be boring! Thank you so much for reading.

Chapter 1

It started with a kiss... We never thought it would come to this!

Sue: Because we have been through so much together, and from such an early age, it seems strange to think there was a time when me and Noel didn't actually know each other.

Even if it was only for a few years.

There are also so many similarities regarding our starts in life that it makes us wonder if we were simply destined to end up together – despite the fact we were born in different parts of the country.

We were both adopted at just a few days old – Noel in Manchester in 1970, me in Kendal, Cumbria, in 1975.

We were both brought up in small families – each having just one older brother. We were both told we were adopted when we were about seven or eight years old. We both took this news in our stride, and just carried on with our happy lives. Me and Noel ended up as near-neighbours once his family had moved to Kendal when he was seven, with Noel initially becoming best mates with my big brother.

We first met when Noel was 11 and I was seven, but it would be a good few years before our lives would dramatically change. Noel was 17 and I was 13 when we had our first kiss – though it does seem weird to revisit those days, and lives that were so incredibly different from the lives we lead today with our enormous family. My mum, Christine, was a care worker, and my dad, Colin, a printer – a compositor, to be precise, for the *Westmorland Gazette* newspaper in Kendal. This was a person who set out the type for printing, in the days before the world went digital crazy. My lovely dad passed away in 2019, but my lovely mum still lives in Kendal – in the same house me and my brother, Stephen, who is two years older than me, grew up in. My first memories are, like most people's, pretty hazy – but I do remember that our house had this little black breakfast bar. It's funny the things that stay with you – while my first memory is of playing out in the garden when I was three. Nothing special – and it was obviously a much quieter garden than the one I became used to as a mum of 22! The only birthday party I can really remember when I was a kid was the one when I must have been about five – it was the birthday party I had after we moved into the house that was pretty much our forever house. It was special to me because my mum had got me this really nice blue and cream-coloured, flowery dress which had lace on the collar. I loved that dress – thanks Mum!

I can always remember getting loads of Christmas presents from Father Christmas, but my dad was one of those people who would rather stay in bed than watch you open your presents. Then again, me and my brother did get up really, really early. My mum used to take us downstairs, and we would play with our presents while dad carried on snoozing. I'd never let Noel do that, but Noel's a big kid at heart so there's no chance he would want to miss out on the action, anyway! One year, I remember getting one of those Sindy Houses. Oh my, I thought it was absolutely amazing. I must have been about seven. Thanks, Father Christmas – and mum and dad! My dear dad never changed – he would always just stay in bed!

Christmases were so quiet, because it was just me and my brother – whereas now, Christmases for us are just crazy, but absolutely amazing as well. They're such a special part of the year for us all, because for so many years the house has just been full of so many excited children. Wrapping paper flying everywhere! It was definitely a lot more civilised when we were younger.

I started going to Brantfield Nursery School in Kendal when I was three or four. Then I went to Heron Hill Primary – and I always remember the little bottles of milk you were given to drink in the morning. I think I was a good pupil. I used to like sewing and art, but I don't know why I liked art so much because I was absolutely rubbish at it. Maybe it didn't bother me because I think I was quite laid-back and chilled as a young girl, and I just got on with things – even if I was no good at them.

Being laid-back and chilled possibly helped me take in the news that I had been adopted. I think I was about seven, and I remember my mum saying to me, 'You're very special because you didn't grow in my tummy, you grew in your other mummy's tummy, but I got to keep you.' And she showed me this bonnet that my birth mum had handed over when she put me up for adoption. But I don't remember feeling anything, really. I just remember thinking, 'Oh, yeah – OK.' And that was it. I think at that age you're just a bit like, 'Yeah, well, whatever...' I didn't really think about it. If I had wanted to see the bonnet and some other bits and pieces that had been given to my adoptive parents then I could have done, because they were just there in a cupboard, but I never asked after that. I think it just shows how settled I was with my mum and dad.

A much bigger deal was going from primary school to secondary school, because the high school we went to had a lower high school and an upper high school. It just seemed so big and different to primary school, and felt so intimidating. But I didn't feel intimidated for long. I can't have, because I did enjoy it. I settled in well and made a lot of good friends. I always hated Maths and Science, though. I didn't mind Geography and loved PE, Domestic Science and Drama. I think I can remember feeling a bit more rebellious the older I got, and dreading some of the lessons I used to go to – because some of the teachers were horrible!

When I looked ahead to the time I'd be ready to leave school, I thought I'd like to be an air hostess. But I was always quite small, so I remember thinking, 'That's probably never going to happen.' I was very sporty and loved running, swimming and gymnastics. I used to do cross country running for the county, and I was very good at gymnastics, too, so I thought I might end up doing something related to sport. I used to watch the gymnasts at the Olympics and thought, 'Oh, I'd love to do that!' An air hostess or an Olympic gymnast – I think they were pretty good dreams to have!

I don't remember ever talking to any of my girlfriends at school about getting married or having kids – they just weren't subjects we were interested in talking about, really. But I think, deep down, I knew I always wanted to get married and have kids – yes, definitely.

Not 22 kids, perhaps, but getting married and having kids – maybe three – would certainly have been at the back of my mind. It would have been a case of 'One day' – I just didn't realise how quickly that day would arrive.

* * *

Noel: Sue's absolutely right – our early lives just seemed to be light years away from what was waiting for us around the corner. We both had good and solid upbringings, but they just seem so quiet – and, yes, peaceful – compared to what would soon become our new normal.

My dad, David, was a buyer for a building supply company. He would buy in the stock for bathrooms and all that sort of stuff. My mum, Val, was a children's nurse when I was younger and, later, a wages clerk. Like Sue, I have an older brother – Ian is 18 months older than me. And like Sue's dad, my mum passed away in 2019. That was a really tough year for us.

My first memory is of me and Ian having our picture taken – sitting on a wall outside our first house. I must have been about three. I can't really remember specific things about my early birthdays, because my birthday is on Christmas Eve and it was always overtaken by the excitement of Christmas Day. But I will never forget one of my brother's birthdays. Mum used to have a multi-coloured feather duster stick and one of the games she played with us involved her pulling a feather out of it and hiding it somewhere. And on this fateful day, one of Ian's friends fell out of the tree where it had been hidden and broke his leg – health and safety was out of the window back then! A favourite Christmas present was a fishing rod, which Father Christmas brought me when I was about five.

But it's funny thinking about those Christmases of my

childhood, when you compare the upbringings me and Sue had to what our kids have had. It's just chalk and cheese. For me and Sue, our childhoods – although we wouldn't have thought this at the time – were relatively quiet. I'd unwrap my presents and take them up to my room and quietly play with them, whereas here it's just chaos all day long. It's strange, because for millions of people all over the country the kind of Christmases me and Sue had when we were kids will be seen as normal – a mum and dad and two kids in the house. But now, we look back and think how weird those Christmas Days were for us, because they were just so quiet. We very quickly got used to the kind of Christmases we have with our very big family, and we just don't see them as being unusual in the slightest. We know, however, that they will seem like anything but normal to the vast majority of the population.

Our kids all have someone to play with on Christmas Day – whereas I had my brother who had his things and wasn't interested in anything I wanted to do, so we just played with our own stuff. It wasn't boring, but it was definitely quieter.

Sue enjoyed her time at nursery, unlike me. I remember going once, and I absolutely hated it. My mum never took me again, because she knew I didn't like it. I think I was a bit of a mummy's boy when I was really young and didn't want to be away from her. Then when I went to primary school – again, I didn't like leaving my mum. I remember getting told off once. There were these little wooden cubes that you used to count with and I was flicking them across the room. I was only in my first year there but the teacher came along, dragged me out of my chair and shook me – and I ended up weeing myself! I didn't want to go home and tell my mum I had been told off because I would have got told off again, so I didn't tell her.

I liked Art and PE at primary school. But I used to hate anything that tested my brain – Maths and English and all that. I wouldn't say I was a shy lad at school – because when you're at school you can't be a mummy's boy. I was always in a big group of friends and was one of the main ones in the group – just a typical boy, really.

I can't remember being sat down and told that I was adopted. But while I can't remember the actual conversation, I do know I would have been about seven or eight. What I do recall is going to primary school after having obviously been told, and telling all my friends, 'I'm adopted' – and suddenly thinking that I'm different and great. But my friends just didn't care – their reaction was like, 'Oh, alright, then.' And that was that. But when you're told something like that at such an early age, I don't think it really means anything to you. The people we called our mum and dad – they were our mum and dad; it was as simple as that.

At secondary school I think I was just like most of the lads – a bit of a pain in the arse for the teachers! I enjoyed doing sports and the Domestic Science lessons, because I liked cooking from an early age. I also liked Pottery and Art. I still hated anything that tested my brain – English and Maths, languages and Science. Oh, I absolutely hated Science. I was OK at school regarding my behaviour. I wasn't a naughty kid – there was maybe one letter sent home for something or other I'd done, but I can honestly say I never skived one day during my whole time at school – not even an afternoon. It wasn't that I liked school so much, I just got on with it.

The first three years of secondary school were all right but I didn't like the next two, and I just kept myself to myself. I had my friends, but it was just a case of turning up, keeping my head down, getting on with the lessons and then going home.

I think I knew from being as young as seven that I wanted to work in a kitchen – be a chef of some description. When I was at primary school, I remember there was once a little cookery lesson – and I brought some ingredients in and baked some cookies or scones, I think. I didn't know why I wanted to be a chef or baker, but it was just something that I seemed to be good at. I used to help my mum and I enjoyed the kitchen life.

I also knew I wanted to get married and settle down. But it wasn't something you talked about with your mates – especially when you were 15 or 16, because they'd think you were a right weirdo, wouldn't they?

* * *

Sue: We started going out with each other on August 4, 1988 – when I was 13 and Noel was 17 – but we met, as near-neighbours, several years before that.

Noel: We lived in cul-de-sacs separated by a ginnel – which you might know as an alley depending on where you're from! I used to play out in what was like a paddock area, but to get to it I had to go through the little street where Sue lived.

Sue: He was a very naughty boy!

Noel: What do you mean? I was a lovely lad!

Anyway, I knew of Sue and her older brother, Stephen, but I didn't really hang around with them initially – I had my own group of friends. It was when we were older that me and Sue became friends, and that was really through Stephen. He was into motorbikes – off-road bikes – and so was I. So that's how I got to know Stephen. So, it was Stephen I was friendly with first, not Sue. Sorry, Sue! I hung around with Stephen for quite a while before I got together with Sue. I would have just sat in

Stephen's room with him and some of our other friends, talking motorbikes – while at the same time Sue would have been in her room with some of her friends. I think we just ended up getting together in a pretty natural way. The first day we were officially boyfriend and girlfriend in our eyes – which we seem to have agreed on, but both of us had to think about it! – was August 4, 1988. Though neither of us can remember if we had our first kiss that day!

Sue: Because we were so young, just 13 and 17, we wouldn't have had a first date in a restaurant or anything like that. Though I do remember, when we were older, going to the restaurant in the Riverside Hotel in Kendal.

Noel: I think you must have been 16 when we went out for our first meal in a restaurant together. I'm guessing, I think that would have been the case.

Sue: Our very first date would have just been hanging around together somewhere. And it wasn't long after that – in September or October, 1988 – that I found out I was pregnant. I was just 13 and couldn't believe it. It was such a big shock.

Noel: For both of us, it was just ... 'Oh shit!'

Sue: But from the word go – from the very moment I realised I was pregnant and told Noel – we knew we were going to keep our child. It didn't matter that I was just 13 and at school and Noel was just 17 and at catering college. We were going to keep the baby and stay together – however difficult that might be and however many obstacles might be in our way. It was as straightforward as that. We were just kids, but we were so determined. We were together and we were going to stay together, and have our baby. It really was a case of just getting on with it. But despite that, there was obviously so much going on in our heads – like, 'Oh my God, how are we going to tell our parents?'

Noel: That was definitely the worst thing about it – knowing that we had to go and tell our parents, and wondering what their reaction would be, especially Sue's mum and dad. I was there when Sue told her mum – but I think your mum knew, didn't she, Sue?

Sue: Yes, I think she did.

Noel: She worked it out, and asked Sue, 'Have you something to tell me?' Sue replied, 'No' – but I thought, 'We've got to go for it here.' So, I said 'Yes' – and then we told her. But, looking back, I think she was alright. She was obviously upset, but I don't think it was as bad as we had feared. She wasn't furious and it wasn't the reaction we perhaps thought it was going to be. Sue's dad was at work at the time. We had talked about it together, before we told anybody and we said that no matter what, we're going to try our best to keep the baby and carry on seeing each other.

We were determined to fight our corner, because we both wanted Sue to have the baby and we certainly didn't want him or her to be adopted – somehow, we wanted to find a way to bring up our child, in spite of everything. But we were very fortunate because in the end – thanks to the response of Sue's mum and dad and my mum and dad – we didn't have to fight our corner. Even though we were very young, they knew we were serious – about each other and about our child – and they knew our minds were made up. In a way, it was as simple as that. And we were so grateful that everyone backed us up, and what I think helped us was Sue's doctor, who told her mum and dad, 'Whatever you do, don't battle against her' – because she knew that kids rebel in those situations. If you try to make them do something, they'll do the opposite – so the doctor's view was to let nature take its course and to go along with our wishes. I think that was the point when people realised just how serious and committed we were – when Sue went to the doctor and said, 'I'm keeping the baby, and that's it.'

Sue: Also, looking back, even if what happened hadn't happened, we would have carried on going out with each other. Even though we were so young, we were so serious about each other. If I hadn't got pregnant at 13, we would have still ended up getting married and having kids together – only later than we actually started!

Noel: Although we were shocked when we found out Sue was pregnant, we weren't thinking, 'Oh my God, that's our lives ruined' or anything like that.

Sue: I feel very lucky because we had so much support from family and friends – although some friends didn't bother with me after I got pregnant. Other friends, though, stuck by me and I still see them today. And I think what we went through made me and Noel stronger as people – and as a couple. We just thought, 'This is a shock, but it's something we've got to deal with together. And we did. Also, not that long after we found out that I was expecting Chris, there was somebody else in my class who got pregnant. But unlike me and Noel, she didn't stay with her boyfriend. I thought it was sad that they ended up splitting up. But me and Noel were always sure that wouldn't happen to us.

Noel: We had so much support from our families, which I think is the main thing that helped us.

Sue: If we didn't have that support, I think things would have been very different.

It was very hurtful when some of my then friends turned their backs on me, because they were really nasty. But it was funny years later when we started doing the TV programmes, because some of the people who had been nasty started coming out of the woodwork – and were wanting to know me again. I wonder if they look back now and think, 'I was really quite nasty' – or do they not even realise how they behaved? I can't remember what was said now, but there was name-calling. Mostly, though, it was just a case of friends deciding not to speak to me again.

Noel: I didn't really experience what Sue experienced. My main friend was Stephen, Sue's brother. There were a few other lads we were friends with, but there were no problems there. And Stephen was fine. He's a really down-to-earth person, and he could see how close me and Sue were – and it was kind of, 'Don't worry about it, you'll be OK.' He was very supportive, like the rest of our families. There was no one pointing the finger at us, and I don't remember any other negativity – apart from what Sue has described regarding some of the girls who used to be her friends.

Sue: I was in what was then known as the third year – of five – at the secondary school, and, really, the school was fine with me. I think it was when I got to about six months pregnant that I started home-schooling. Then Chris was born in May and I went back to school in September. And when I went back – and what kind of made things better for me in a way – there was that other girl who was the same age as me now having her baby. That just made things seem a lot easier and then in the last school year there were other girls who became pregnant.

My mum helped us so much. She used to do care work, but she gave her job up that September when I went back, so she could look after Chris while I was at school. She did try working nights, but she absolutely hated it.

Noel: I wasn't in any bother with any of the authorities because I think, back then, it was all down to your mums and dads and what they thought – and they decided not to take it any further, but to just help us through it all. I think it may have been different if I was one of these lads who didn't hang around – 'You're pregnant, see you later!' – but that was never going to be the case. I think someone, somewhere may have had to report what happened – the doctor, maybe – but there weren't any repercussions, and I think that was because my intention was to stay with Sue and support her and our child. There was no knock on the door from anyone saying I was in big trouble. What happened back then has obviously been brought up again in recent years, after we became known by going on television. People have inevitably talked about the situation and it has been written about in the newspapers and discussed on social media. There has been a lot of focus on it and, in a way, it was probably worse for us than when it actually happened. So many people, who we don't know, have given their opinions. But we were both kids – it was not as if I was 10 or 15 years older than Sue. For a lot of people, though, things are just black and white and you are tarnished with the same brush as other people in totally different situations. We were young and we were daft, but we were a couple and we continued as a couple.

Sue: It's more the effects that all the bad comments might have on the kids. Particularly Chris. Because when people talk today about me and Noel and what happened all those years ago, it now affects Chris as well – it's not just about us anymore. We were being dragged back to it, but for Chris it was the first time he had to face people talking about it.

Noel: And once it's out there on the internet, it's there forever. If Chris wants to look and find things like that, he could do – as everyone in the family could. But I think the kids now know not to go searching. But yes, some of the comments from people were brutal – that I should have been arrested and things like that. Even though I was just 17 – still a kid, including in the eyes of the law. But it doesn't bother me. People will say what they like. I don't care what they say.

Sue: And Noel, like me, was still in education at the time.

Noel: I was at catering college when I found out we were having Chris. I had to quit that, because I had to start earning money. I found a job that paid a decent wage, working in a Gateway supermarket. I had told my tutor at college – Mr Lawson – I was going to have to leave. He was a bit upset and asked me what I wanted to do. He very kindly rang Gateway for me and then reported back, saying, 'You can either be a trainee butcher or trainee baker, what do you fancy doing?' So I said, 'I'll be a trainee baker, then.' And that's how I ended up in the baking trade, having previously spent some time as a chef on a work placement in a hotel. It was a tough time for us in so many ways. But now I can look back and think there have been a lot of people who have stuck up for us along the way, and they are now able to point out that we've been together for more than 35 years and had 22 kids.

Sue: Our lives changed so much back then, and so quickly. We got a council house together in 1991. I was 16 then and Noel was 20, and I was able to leave home and be with Noel, who had been in a flat. It also meant my mum could go back to her care work as I had left school and was able to look after Chris with Noel. But it's funny looking back to the time we got our first place together. I had always wanted to go to Florida and my mum would say, 'No, it's too expensive.' Then me and Chris moved out and into the council house with Noel – and pretty much that day my mum and dad went on holiday to Florida! To be fair, it was around the time of the Gulf War and I think they got a bargain holiday – but still, I couldn't forgive them for that (I'm joking!)

Noel: And we have certainly made up for it since, with our own trips to Florida with the kids!

Sue: After having Chris, when we talked about the future it was talking about us getting married and about getting better jobs because we had so little money – that was more the conversation between us, rather than talking at that point about how many kids we might have.

Noel: That would be the next stage – it was more a case then of trying to get ourselves on firmer ground, regarding money and getting married.

Sue: I was 17 when we got married – on September 26, 1992 – and I remember my dad had to write a letter to the vicar, giving his permission. The vicar was Peter Smith, who was our old Maths teacher.

Noel: But there was no talk of us going to Gretna Green to be married – we wanted the traditional white wedding in a church. And although we got married in September, it wasn't until December that we went on our honeymoon to Gambia – because it was two weeks for the price of one in that month! Chris stayed at home with Sue's mum and dad – and, after the honeymoon, we didn't go away again on a holiday on our own for another 30 years. Though we did have the odd night away together now and again.

Sue: It hadn't been our plan to have such a big family. We had always said, in the early days, that we would have three kids. And then we thought, 'Ah, let's have another one.' And that kept on happening!

Noel: You enjoyed being pregnant, didn't you?

Sue: Yeah. And it's so lovely to have children close together so they're quite similar in age. Also, I just think there's something really special about having a big family. I couldn't imagine not having a big family now.

Noel: We sometimes think, 'If we had had just two kids, what would we be doing with ourselves now?'

Sue: I just couldn't even imagine that – I couldn't imagine not having such a big family. We both just love it. It was usually when the most recent baby was between six months to a year old that I would get broody and be thinking about having another one.

Noel: We've already said we were addicted to having children, and we both feel very fortunate that we have been able to have so many.

Sue: People mention the sleep deprivation, but you did just get used to it and it never made me think, 'Oh, that's it. I can't have any more kids.'

Noel: The only problem we ever came across was with Chloe, because she had colic and it was just hell every night with her crying and us desperately trying to get her to sleep.

Sue: We tried taking her out in the car and driving around, but nothing seemed to work.

Noel: But that was the only time. And even then, we never thought, 'Right, we're not having any more now.' When Sue was expecting our ninth child, James, I did have a vasectomy (which we'll talk about in greater detail later). There was a bit of peer pressure, and remarks being made – which I think started after we'd had five kids – so we eventually caved in and went for it. It wasn't a question of people saying, 'You should go and have the snip' – it was more jokes and hints. But then, from the day I had the vasectomy, we totally regretted it. And later, after I had the vasectomy reversal, it wasn't a case of, 'Right, we'll stop when we get to 15' or whatever.

Sue: After having and losing Alfie, who was stillborn and our 17th child (he will have his own chapter dedicated to his memory), we were so scared of going through that again, and thought, initially, that we couldn't try to have any more. It was just an awful time. Absolutely heartbreaking. And then when I was pregnant the next time, with Hallie, it was so mentally draining because you were constantly worried something might go wrong. I think when we lost Alfie, we realised just how much we had taken having children for granted – and when you do go through something like we did with Alfie, you learn just how common it is. But I know I have been so lucky overall, because, apart from Alfie, all my pregnancies have been straightforward.

Although we did have some people tell us we should have stopped at a certain number, we surround ourselves with friends who are like-minded and have quite a few children of their own.

We've got friends who have 10 children, and five – so they know all about big families and the chaos involved. Whereas if you had no children or one child and came to our house, you would be like 'Aaaaagh!' I don't think they'd be able to cope with it all. It is chaotic, but we love it – and there has only been one point in our marriage where I thought we might be in danger of getting divorced. That was in 2001 after we had taken out a huge loan on a second shop (more of which later in the book).

Noel: Me and Sue have always had our regular date nights. I think they're really important for a married couple, especially when you've got this much going on in your lives. You've got to be able to find the time to talk to each other as a couple, rather than just talking in baby language or the language of teenagers. People sometimes ask me what the secret is to a long and happy marriage – just say 'Yes' to whatever she says!

Sue: No, I think it's give and take, isn't it? And keep talking and listening to each other – and never go to bed on an argument.

Noel: Whatever she said!

Sue: We're also asked about the secret to being a good mum and dad. You do need to have a lot of patience, don't you?

Noel: And try not to get too stressed.

Sue: Yes, definitely, because I think if you are stressed then that will rub off on the kids.

Noel: When we had Chris, I think we were your typical helicopter parents who just worried about everything. But as you go on and have more kids, then you realise what you do need to worry about and what you don't need to worry about.

Sue: And even if you have a very big family, you just know instinctively when a certain child needs your particular attention, and you take the time out – and spend it with the one who, at that point in their lives, needs your time. You can always tell when there is something going on with one of your children – they can never hide anything; you just know.

Noel: You just pick up on the bad vibes if something isn't quite right.

Sue: We've been lucky enough to have grandchildren as well, and that's obviously a different thing.

Noel: It's definitely different. You can spoil them a bit more and not worry about the consequences – send them home hyped up! But I think the love is the same for them. It's just nice when you're absolutely knackered at the end of the day, to be able to then say, 'There you go – have your child back!'

Sue: I think when we're on holiday and are able to properly unwind, there is time then to take a minute and look around at everyone all together and think, 'Wow, we are so lucky.'

Noel: And at Christmas, when they're all here – and if you take a moment to step back and look at everyone in the room, kids and grandkids, you just smile and think, 'This is great!'

Sue: I definitely think having all these kids has kept us feeling young. They are all so different. I always say there are so many different characters in the house.

Noel: There are some that are similar in some ways – Heidie is very much like Phoebe was when she was younger, and some of the boys are similar.

Sue: When I look at our family today, I occasionally think about the doubters – and the people who were nasty or turned their backs on me when I was expecting Chris. My message to them would be, 'Look at us now, and what we have got. We are still together, more than 35 years on, with 22 kids, 10 grandchildren and two successful businesses.' We didn't doubt ourselves at the start and we've always had the mindset that if you want something badly enough you can get it.

Noel: Yes, we have had some bad times, but we have also been so incredibly fortunate. Me and Sue are so proud of our family, and so grateful. I've no regrets – and there is still so much to look forward to.

Chapter 2

Along came...
Chris, then Sophie,
then Chloe, then
Jack, and then...

Christopher
Born May 7, 1989

Sue: Wow – it's hard to believe it when I look back now. Here I was, still a child, myself – just a little over 14 years old – having my first baby. I suppose, in a way, it doesn't seem real today. But it wasn't like that at the time, possibly because I had nine months to get my head around the fact I was going to be a mum – and also because me and Noel had fought so hard for our son, Chris. Our ages at the time – Noel was now 18 – were not as big an issue for us as they might have been for other people. The simple fact was that, even though we hadn't planned that it would happen so early, we were now parents – mum and dad to our own baby, and we couldn't have been happier even though the road we were on was not an easy one. But while we were short of money and couldn't yet live together as a family, we knew this would not always be the case.

My first pregnancy was very smooth – no problems at all. Until, that is, it came to the labour! It was a 26-hour labour – really difficult. That was the worst labour I've had – my very first. But obviously it didn't put me off! Chris was 6lb 8oz – one of our smaller ones. And when he was born, he didn't really have much hair – he just had a little bit of dark hair. Everything was new to us, of course. We had a lot of help from my mum and dad in those early days with Chris – both sets of parents were really, really good. But the early years were a bit different to what they were with the others – because Chris was our first and because of the difficult circumstances we were in because of our ages.

Noel: Our first child – such a special time! Me and Sue had already made people realise how serious we were about each other. We had explained that we were going to stay together and bring up our baby as best we could – although we knew we couldn't live together at first and would also need plenty of support. Then Sue leaving school at 16 while I swapped college for a job underlined just how quickly we had grown up and happily accepted our responsibilities.

With Chris being our first – well, you spoil them rotten, don't you? And then regret it later in life! And you're mollycoddling them and fussing over them, because it's all new to you.

Sue: I think we went through about four prams with Chris.

Noel: Easily more than that, Sue!

Sue: I just loved the different prams you could get. I'd buy one, then see another I liked – so I'd sell the first one, move it on and get another. And that continued. I admit it, I do have a pram obsession and I think that's when it all started. Chris was no problem – he was quite a chilled and placid baby and toddler. He was always fine when we took him to toddler groups and my mum, who helped me look after him, didn't have any problems with him, either. He was a really good child to look after – which, being our first, we were very grateful for.

Noel: As a baby, he really was a good one – he slept through from quite early on. As he got older and his character traits began to come through, I think he was just a typical little lad, really – he was cheeky and, like so many kids the older they get, he pushed the boundaries to see how far he could go. But he wasn't horrible or rude or anything, just your normal, cheeky lad. He liked football from an early age, and still likes football to this day. He did a bit of fell-running with me when he was old enough, and was quite an outdoors type of lad – nowadays, of course, kids are just staring at a screen from an early age. I remember we used to go out for a lot of walks with him, and he really enjoyed doing that.

Sue: I remember a funny thing with Chris. He was a bit obsessed with collecting the Pokemon cards when he was little – he had this big stash of them. Him and his mate kept going to the local shop to get these cards.

Noel: Yeah, and him and his friend had a den around the corner – they would only have been around six or seven – and I remember once when it was time for him to come in, about 6pm, we went to go and find him. We just saw him walking past and counting all these cards. I then went into his den and it was just carpeted with these Pokemon cards – there were just loads of them! Anyway, it turned out he and his friend had been, erm, borrowing them from the shop – so we dragged him round there and the shopkeeper said, 'Oh, it's not him who's been taking them, it's his friend.'

Sue: Oh, my word! When he got rumbled for that he knew he was in trouble!

Noel: That was the first thing he ever did that was naughty, I suppose. I also remember he used to have this strawberry birth mark on his bum when he was younger and he used to proudly show that off to people now and again!

Sue: He did so well with his running – it wasn't just with you, Noel, was it, because he'd do well at school with his cross country running. He did go to one primary school in Kendal which he absolutely hated.

One of the teachers really had it in for him, it seemed to Chris, and he didn't do very well at all at that school – it just wasn't for him. But then he switched schools and he just seemed to thrive. But he looks back at that time at the other primary school and I think he was traumatised by it. But you don't realise the effect some bad experience like that can have on them when they're that young. He basically didn't want to go to that school because he felt he was being bullied – it was terrible. But fortunately, overall, Chris has always been quite a happy-go-lucky person. He always had a lot of friends at school and didn't really let things get to him – it was just that one incident.

Noel: His teenage years – well, you always dread them as a parent, especially with a lad, and Chris was obviously our first experience of that, and we weren't sure what to expect. But he was always alright, I think, looking back – maybe a typical teenager, wanting specific things. I remember with Chris, he wanted to have Rockport boots – they were very important to him. But luckily, with teenagers back then, it wasn't so much about having the latest fashions – Nike tops and so on – as it is now. He wanted certain tracksuit bottoms and these shoes, but he wasn't overly bothered about other things. And the group of friends he used to hang around with were all fine, we never had any trouble there.

As teenagers go, Chris was a nice lad! You'd have the times when he would just grunt rather than talk – but that's the same with all teenagers, as we would later find out! But as soon as Chris left school, he was straight into work. He left school on the Friday and began work on the Monday, and he's been in work ever since. He's done all sorts. He worked in a glass factory, making double-glazing units. He worked at Jaguar Land Rover – powder-coating parts, I think it was – and he's done scaffolding. Now he's working in a warehouse. He loves working but you'd never get him on a till in Asda or anything like that – he likes to be behind-the-scenes. He'd work at Asda, but as long as it was in the warehouse. He can put his hand to anything. He's also given us three grandchildren, and he loves his kids to bits. And they're lovely kids, as well.

Sue: Chris lived away with his former partner – in Northamptonshire – for several years, from when he was about 26 or 27. But he's back living here now, which is great for us. He returned in the early part of 2023.

Noel: As much as you do want your kids to leave when they grow up, when they do you then think, 'Oh, I wish they were back here!'

Sue: Also, he wasn't just down the road. It was like a three-hour drive, so it was a long way and it took quite a bit of getting used to for us.

Noel: We didn't see him for months on end – because he was busy working, we were busy working, and busy with the rest of the family. And it was a long way to go for just the weekend. It had to be texts and phone calls for long periods of time, just because of the distance.

Sue: Chris hasn't been on the TV show much – part of that has been because he hasn't been around here for a large part of it, but also he's not keen on being in the limelight, just like his younger brother, Jack. Which is fine because we'd never force any of them to be more involved than they want to be.

With Chris, because he's the closest to us in age, it's nice to be able to go out and socialise with him.

Noel: Because we are closer in age, he's someone you can have a conversation with – someone who's like a friend, as well as being your child.

Sue: And he's absolutely brilliant with all his siblings.

Sophie Rose
Born December 13, 1993

Sue: It was so special, having my first girl – my first daughter. I think, having had Chris, we really wanted a girl next. But back then you couldn't find out what you were having, so when she was born it was lovely.

And it was a really easy pregnancy again, while, unlike with Chris, the labour was quite quick – almost too quick as it turned out. I remember my waters breaking in bed and then us racing to the hospital. She was born in Helme Chase Maternity Unit in Kendal. There was an old Helme Chase and a new Helme Chase

– and the day Sophie was born was the day the old maternity unit was moving over to the new one, so they were getting everything out of boxes. I think Sophie was just the second baby to be born there – and I actually thought she was going to be born in the car, because things were moving so quickly after my waters broke. It was really touch and go.

Noel: And we couldn't get in at first, could we?

Sue: That's right, I remember us pressing that buzzer! Then I remember a problem with the lift, which wasn't working properly. Oh God! But fortunately we got there in the end and everything was OK, but it was a close-run thing – from my waters breaking to Sophie arriving was only an hour. She was 6lb 14oz.

Noel: Looking back, it was funny because there were these big cardboard boxes in the room filled with things that would normally be on a shelf or put away somewhere. But they were still unpacking! Sue got settled, though, and Sophie made her entrance, and it was all fine. And yes, I was just as keen as Sue to have our first daughter. I think when you have a boy or a girl, you want the next one to be the opposite. It was a lovely surprise for us when she appeared – there she was, a little girl and our first daughter, to go along with our son, Chris.

We had been living together – me, Sue and Chris – as a family for well over two years by the time Sophie was born. It was different, bringing her up as a baby – and not least for Sue, because she could put her in all these frilly dresses! That's what you were really looking forward to, wasn't it?

Sue: We definitely felt more confident straight away, bringing up Sophie, compared to how we were with Chris.

Noel: Definitely. Because by then I think we knew what a cry was that was just whingeing, and what was a cry that needed your attention. And if Sophie got a rash, you'd think, 'I've been through this before, this is nothing to worry about.' It's like with any parent – you've had your first and just don't know what anything is and what you need to do. You have to learn from experience.

Sue: But luckily, like Chris, Sophie was an easy baby. She was quite a chubby baby and I remember the health visitor coming out to me when she was about 10 months old and she'd just started crawling – and because she was quite chubby, the health visitor said, 'Oh, you need to put her on a diet.' And I said, 'I'm not putting her on a diet. There's no way. She'll lose weight when she starts walking.' Looking back now, you just think, 'What an absolutely ridiculous thing to say!' But yes, she loved her baby food – and Farley's Rusks!

Noel: She also had a tendency to put snails in her mouth – she'd have one in each cheek! She'd suck on them before you had the chance to take them out of her mouth. Oh, it was horrible – all that slime!

Sue: Oh my God, that was terrible. They were really, really sticky, weren't they?

Noel: I also remember the time we went to tuck her in one night and she was blue. She'd helped herself to some Miracle-Gro plant food and covered herself in it! But it didn't work, because she was only tiny!

Sue: We took her up to the hospital and they were laughing and joking – saying, 'She'll be absolutely fine, but she might have a bit of a growth spurt!' That was so funny – but only looking back, not before we got her to the hospital!

Noel: Another time, Sue had this glass of wine that had been by her – but then it disappeared. The next thing we know, Sophie is running around and bouncing off the chairs and running into walls and things!

Sue: I'd left it on the side – she must have been three or four at the time, and was able to get her hands on it when I wasn't looking. There was only a little bit in it, but she drank it and it obviously had an effect. It was hilarious.

Noel: We called the hospital and asked them what we should do – they said, 'Don't worry about it, she'll sleep it off.' So yes, Sophie was a very inquisitive and curious child, which led to her getting into one or two scrapes.

Sue: She was quite difficult at school, I must admit.

Noel: She was fine in primary school.

Sue: But when she got to her last few years, at secondary school, that was quite hard – I remember she was really upset because she didn't get on with this one teacher and she wasn't allowed to go to her prom, because this teacher didn't like her. She wasn't really naughty, just a bit mischievous, I would say. But she's never got over the fact that this teacher wouldn't let her go to the prom. I think the problem was – as far as the teacher was concerned – Sophie was always very chatty.

Noel: Oh, she was a chatterbox with her friends.

Sue: And teachers don't like that, do they?

Noel: She was just talking when she shouldn't have been talking. She wasn't rude and didn't answer back or anything.

Sue: She was just always chatting – and she's never changed, because she's like that now!

Noel: Like Chris, Sophie was also good at running – all the kids have been good at that, really, so this will come up a lot. She used to run for the primary school. There was also this one race, it was in Lancaster, and there were a few hundred in it – and I'm looking out for her, thinking, 'She'll be halfway, at least,' and she just came past me. She was about 10th in this really big field of runners. I couldn't believe it. She was about 10 or 11 at the time.

She doesn't run anymore, though – too busy being a mum and working part-time.

Sue: Sophie's a very caring person, and she's always looking out for everyone else. She's just a really caring and lovely person.

Noel: She's another one who has left school, gone straight into work and never looked back since. She used to work for us in the bakery, then went off to work in maintenance at Heysham nuclear power station – and she's still there now. She's quite good at DIY, and enjoys decorating and things like that. She's very practical and will get stuck in no matter what it is. Sophie also gave us our first three grandchildren, which was lovely.

Chloe Anne
Born July 31, 1995

Sue: Another easy pregnancy, I'm delighted to say! And there were no problems with the labour. Chloe was 7lb 2oz – but to me, she was the dinkiest one, because she had really long, skinny legs, and long fingers. We always used to joke that she would be a pianist.

When she was born, it was a really hot summer – one of the hottest on record, I think – and I remember, when she was only a few days old, going to this place called Mardale in the Lake District. It was a really hot day – I'll never forget it, because it was one of the hottest days I can ever remember. Maybe it wasn't the best idea to go there! We were glad to get home that day.

But the big problem with Chloe as a baby was the colic she had, from about seven weeks old. It was absolutely horrendous. There was another mum who lived up the street from us who had her baby at the same time. I remember we were on our way to Asda once, and she was saying her baby had colic as well. So, we went to buy this liquid to give our babies in these pipette things, but it didn't work at all. It was just an absolutely terrible time. Poor Chloe!

Noel: It was gripe water back then, wasn't it?

Sue: That's right. And Chloe's colic probably lasted about three months – which is a really long time. The crying used to start at the exact same time every evening, and it would just carry on and carry on. There was nothing we could do to help.

Noel: She wouldn't be able to settle at night, and eventually we just had to leave her – she hates that idea, even to this day she'll tell us, 'You abandoned me!' But we just had to let her settle herself.

Sue: We used to take her out for a ride in the car and she'd fall asleep – but then she'd wake up and we would have to put her in a quiet place in the living room and just wait until she was able to go off to sleep again. It never used to take her too long but she used to get so frustrated with herself that you just couldn't do anything. It was awful, and thankfully none of our other kids ever had that. But once she got through the colic stage, Chloe was fine.

Noel: She always got her head down in school and just got on with it. She did really well at school and enjoyed herself there – primary and secondary. Like the others, she was good at running – she loved her cross country. Chloe was a very quiet child and I don't recall there being any dramas with her at all. She is a very strong-willed person and if she's right about something, she'll let you know she's right!

Sue: And if she's wrong, she'll still be right! I think we first noticed this part of her personality when she was in high school.

And she's just carried it on – she's very much like me, really. She's very strong-willed.

Noel: She reminds me of my late mum, too. She's quite bossy. When I was younger, I remember all my mum had to do was look at me a certain way, and I knew I'd better start behaving. I think Mila – Chloe's daughter – might get to know that look!

Sue: When Chloe has babysat for us, she has taken no messing!

Noel: And Chloe has always been a good worker. She first worked at the bakery for us on a Saturday when she was at school. And she later worked for us before going to university in Plymouth.

Sue: She had a year there in digs that the university provided, but was finding the course really difficult – it was a teaching course which would have led to her being a primary school teacher – and she was missing home. She then managed to get a place at Lancaster University, just down the road from us. She did a year there and was going to go into a third year of the course but decided it was too hard and she didn't want to carry on with it. I think she just lost interest in it, really.

Noel: Then she came back to us, but in between that and coming back to work at the bakery she went to France to work as an au pair in one of the ski resorts. But that didn't pan out so well. She was supposed to be there for six months or something, but was only there for a few weeks before breaking her ankle after falling awkwardly as she was walking along a pavement. She came back here and didn't return. But she was also going to go to Australia for a year with a friend – Chloe was all up for it, but her friend backed out and they never actually went. Chloe has shown, through all of that, she is quite adventurous and is prepared to try different things – but I think she's totally settled down now.

Jack Richard
Born April 9, 1997

Sue: When Jack arrived, we were quite the family – a family of four children, two boys and two girls. And me and Noel were still so young – I had just turned 22, and Noel was 26. I suppose you could say we still had plenty of time to have plenty more children! Jack was an easy pregnancy and easy birth, and he was 7lb 6oz when he was born. He had blond hair – he's always been quite fair, Jack. Most of our kids are dark, bar Jack and Casper. Jack was quite an easy baby, overall, but he could be quite a whingey baby at times. He demanded a lot of attention, I must admit. Chris, Sophie and Chloe could quite happily entertain themselves by playing with each other, whereas Jack had to have my attention constantly. But growing up, he's always been quite placid and quiet, and he did really well in school. We've never had any problems with Jack at all, have we?

Noel: No, he's as good as gold is Jack, very easy-going.

Sue: He's got quite a wicked sense of humour. He is quiet and a bit shy but his sense of humour is very on point – his one-liners are great. He isn't really bothered about being filmed for the TV show. If they say, 'Can we just borrow you to do this little bit?' he'll do it, but he's not really interested in being on TV. He'll happily stay in the background.

Noel: He'll sit and talk to the camera crew but as soon as that camera is switched on, he's off! He's just a very chilled-out guy.

Sue: And he's a bit of an entrepreneur. He likes buying and selling on eBay in his spare time, and he's quite good at it.

Noel: Jack wasn't really a sporty guy growing up – he was more into computers. He'll watch football on TV – he'll watch Liverpool – but taking part in sports was never a big thing for him.

Sue: When he was little, we used to call him – and we still do, actually – 'Junk Food Jack.'

Noel: He loves chocolate!

Sue: He just loves any junk food – and he's never changed from that, really.

Noel: Although he's not generally sporty, he did go through a spell of playing football for a club – but they were rubbish! I think it was Heysham Blue Stars – and if they came away losing seven-nil it was a good result! He just got sick of it and said, 'I'm not doing this anymore.' When he played, he was good. But the problem was he never used to get picked to start. He'd have to travel for half an hour or so and then end up just playing for 10 minutes. He just lost interest.

After school, Jack went to college because he wanted to be an accountant – he got in with an accounting company who he did all this training with. But then something happened when the college said he had to start paying for something, so he could no longer afford it. He's with us now, working at the bakery, but he's another one who found some work at the power station – working on the outage. They clean everything and paint it and it's just silly money while they're doing it. But it's going to be the bakery long-term, I think.

Chapter 3

Pie Heaven,
'Divorce' Hell

Sue

Things were so good for us at the start of 1999. We had four children, were expecting a fifth – we'll be talking about Daniel, and others, in the next chapter – and, with Noel having picked up so much experience working for others, felt we were now in a position to open a shop and be our own bosses.

We opened for business in Heysham, which is about 30 miles south of Kendal – where we were brought up and still living – on February 12, 1999, and things went well right from the start.

Daniel arrived in March 1999. Then, in October 2000, with business still booming, Luke, our sixth child, was born. We then took the decision to open a second shop – and this one would be in Kendal, the place which meant the most to us. I'd spent all my life there and Noel had lived there since he was seven. Everything seemed to be falling into place, and the idea of having a shop in Kendal – a place we couldn't have known any better – just seemed perfect. It was like a dream come true for us – but, sadly, the dream turned into a complete and utter nightmare. It turned out that it was the worst move we could have possibly made. It's difficult now to even think about it, let alone write about it.

Looking back, one part of what was an unfolding disaster was the fact that in those days you could get finance so easily. You really could just sign your life away. And we were certainly signing ourselves up to a load of debt.

I think we were also lulled into a false sense of security because of the first shop doing well. Actually, it was doing more than that – it was thriving. So, if you put everything together, expanding the business by getting a second shop just seemed like the natural thing to do – and Kendal the obvious place to open it. But we were heading for hell on earth – though I think if we had gone for a different site in the town, things could well have worked out very differently.

The rent for the place we chose was a ridiculous amount of money and the business rates were crazy, because it was in the centre of town. You were always going to have to take a hell of a lot of money to even recover your costs. The Kendal shop actually did OK for the first few months, after we opened in December 2000 – but little did we know that disaster was lurking around the corner for the country's farming and tourism industries. They were about to be hit by foot-and-mouth disease, which affected Cumbria really badly – including scores of businesses, like our new shop. The outbreak of the disease lasted from February 2001 – just a couple of months after we opened in Kendal – until the end of September 2001, by which time we had no choice but to shut up shop in the town. It had got to the point where the business in Heysham was having to take a big hit, because we were having to divert money from it into the Kendal shop.

We were thinking, 'This is not good, and if we don't get out of this now, we could end up losing everything.' We didn't stand a chance, really – especially when you factor in foot-and-mouth. But it had been a bit of a slow process after it first started. I'd say for the first six weeks or so of foot-and-mouth, we didn't realise how bad things were going to get. Our seventh child, Millie, was born on August 29, 2001 – and we pulled out of the Kendal business when she was only a few weeks old, so we were trading there for less than a year.

It was just really bad timing – nightmare timing. No one could have seen foot-and-mouth coming. That summer of 2001 was just awful – everyone just stayed away. Kendal was a ghost town. I remember having these conversations with Noel just before Millie was born – and we were constantly saying, 'How long do we leave things before we have to pull out?'

At the time, we were thinking, 'Are we going to have to sell our house?' We couldn't get out of our three-year lease on the second shop – initially, I think the landlord had wanted £25,000 from us, which we couldn't afford because of the amount of debt we had taken on. Noel eventually did a deal with him for a lesser amount, but we still ended up having to raise money on the house. On the positive side, although we were still left with a lot of debt, we didn't lose the roof over our heads.

The business in Heysham had been having to carry the one in Kendal because it wasn't bringing in the money, and we really did think we might end up having to sell our house. We had so many bills – we had car finance, as we bought a van to take things between the businesses, and we had credit cards. We were thinking, 'We've got to prioritise our mortgage' and then any bills we can still afford to pay after the mortgage, we'd pay them next. It was absolutely horrendous, and it was a turning point in our lives – because we agreed from that moment on never to get finance for anything.

We learned the hard way by getting ourselves into that position, and we've always said to the kids that they're far better off paying for something outright if they can afford it. We tell them, 'Don't get anything on finance because you just don't know what's around the corner.' In one respect, it taught us valuable life lessons that we still live by today – that you don't overstretch yourselves and take on things that you may end up not being able to afford. I reckon we must have lost around £40,000 to £45,000 in total on the whole Kendal nightmare – it's just depressing to think about it. It took us a good few years to pay all that off and to get straight again.

We took out that loan against the house over, I think, a five-year period. It was such an awful time in our lives – we used to go to bed at night thinking about the debt we were in, we'd wake up during the night thinking about the debt we were in and we'd wake up in the morning and immediately start thinking about the debt we were in. And, all the time, you're wondering how the hell you are ever going to get out of it. It really was like hell on earth for us. I could never ever think about going back to something like that – there is no way I would take on debt like that again.

The whole thing took its toll on me and Noel, and our marriage. Yes, we did stick together and yes, we got through it – working really, really hard to keep a roof over our heads, food in our kids' bellies and to pay our bills off. But it was a really shitty time. I just kept thinking, 'There's no way out of this, and I really don't see how our marriage can survive it.'

We were obviously in it together – it wasn't just one of us – so we would have been sick of the sight of the second shop because of the horrendous problems and debt associated with it, and sick of the sight of each other. I think it was probably coming more from me than Noel – Noel is the sort of person who would just take things. But at the time I would have been thinking, 'Oh my God, I just hate you!'

There were a few times when I was shouting at Noel that I wanted the whole business gone – 'Put the first shop up for sale and let's just walk away from everything.' I'm so glad that Noel was a bit more patient and suggested we give it a bit longer. Some people have said me and Noel don't seem to have big arguments on the TV programme. And it's true, we don't. But I genuinely do think when you've hit rock bottom and been through a year like we went through with that shop in Kendal, and your marriage has gone through that, what else can happen? So, I think, we've been quite chilled since then. But looking back now, I genuinely don't know how we got through that time. I think it was a case of just making sure the mortgage was paid every month – that was the absolute priority – and then we would pay the other bills after that.

We were lucky in that the original business had always been really steady, so we could always rely on a certain amount of money coming in from that. The Heysham shop wasn't seasonal, but if it had been more like the Kendal one things would have ended very differently. But even so, there were still definitely some days when I really did think, 'That's it, I'm leaving the business and Noel, I just can't do it anymore.' Then other days we were fine. There was just more pressure on certain days – like if another bill arrived, and you were left thinking, 'How on earth are we ever going to be able to pay this as well?'

Looking back now, I can see that we would never, ever have called it a day but when you're in that highly-pressurised and highly-stressed moment, you're just not thinking straight. When you're in the middle of something like that it's just very hard to see a way out of it. But we did learn so much from the experience.

We always made sure we didn't get to that point where we got a bad credit rating and would have to go bankrupt. We always paid our bills whenever we could and did our very best to keep on top of things – even if it meant our first business having to take a big hit. We did, somehow, manage by the skin of our teeth to get out of it – even if it did all have a knock-on effect on the Heysham shop. Today, we still can't face going down that street in Kendal. My mum lives in Kendal and Noel's dad lives in Kendal, but I don't ever go to the shops there now.

The whole experience made us wiser. And what doesn't kill you makes you stronger. I think you have to have a very strong marriage to get through something like that – and we've always had a very strong marriage. We certainly went through hell – but, thankfully, no divorce. And the great thing is, as you'll see detailed later in the book, there was another generous helping of Pie Heaven on the way for our business, which we're still enjoying today!

Noel

Just to rewind, I'd been working for 10 years or so – in supermarket in-store bakeries and independent bakeries – and felt the time was right for us to take the big leap of going into business ourselves. In early 1999, the chance came to take on a well-established shop and bakery – Faraday's in Heysham. We moved there from Kendal the following year – the move to Morecambe, two or three miles north of Heysham, came four years after that.

There was a bakery attached to the shop, and we made and sold pies, sandwiches and cakes. Trade was good, and we couldn't have been happier with our lives at home or at work. Everything seemed to be going well – but that might have been part of the problem. We probably assumed things would go just as well with the second shop as they were going with the first. Why wouldn't they?

Now, with the benefit of hindsight, I can see some of the problems we didn't think about at the time. We were still pretty young, for a start. In late 2000, I was about to celebrate my 30th birthday, while Sue was 25. Also, it was me, especially, who didn't think things through enough or put a proper business plan together for the second shop. I didn't do all the sums properly, about how well it might do – or how badly it might do. In addition to this, Sue had relatives who had their own sandwich shop in Kendal and they were giving us information about how successful it was and how much money they took, so we were going off those figures.

All of this led to me marching ahead – thinking it was defi-nitely a good idea to do it. And it was definitely me who was the keenest to do it at that point, even though we hadn't had the first shop for that long. Sue was a lot more cautious. I was just young and stupid, basically – that was my excuse. Then again, Sue was even younger than me and she wasn't being stupidly over-optimistic about things like I was!

It was basically a case of, 'Yeah, give me the forms – I'll sign them.' I think the main thing behind me making the decision pretty quickly – and probably recklessly – was the point about the second shop being in Kendal. It had such a great pull for us emotionally, and so the idea of having a business there really appealed. It was just one of those things where, for sentimental reasons, you would just love to see your name above a shop in the town. We also thought that, because of our history with the place, the Kendal shop would probably go on to be our main business. The shop was at 44, Highgate – we went there a while ago to do some filming for the TV programme and viewers saw that it was then a mobile phone shop. But at the time of writing, it's empty again. Maybe it's just cursed.

We rented the premises, which we had a three-year lease on, and leased all the equipment we needed for it. So, in the end, the outgoings just added up to stupid money. The rent, I think, was £20,000 a year, and the rates were about £12,000 a year. That was just so we could open the door. Then we were leasing the shop counters – I can't remember how much they were, but probably around £300 to £400 a month because it was top of the range stuff we got. Then there was the electricity and the wages to pay out. Our annual outgoings before we even sold a single sandwich, cake or pie were probably getting towards £40,000.

Then came foot-and-mouth!

As soon as they started saying to people 'Don't go to the Lake District – keep away,' that's when things went totally downhill.

But the thing is, Kendal isn't actually in the Lake District, it's on the edge. A lot of people didn't realise that, and so they didn't realise they could have come to Kendal and there would have been no problems whatsoever. I suppose the thing is, if you're holidaying in the Lakes you might go through Kendal or visit it for a day out. But the problem was people just weren't going there.

We started to notice a reduction in footfall – and the takings were obviously less as a result of fewer people being around the town. That was gradual at first but, sadly, it just got worse and worse. We suffered from a combination of things, really. It was a perfect storm for us. We agreed to pay far too much to trade from there, we had that sentimental pull of Kendal, while the success of the first shop gave us the confidence to expand at that time – even though I was too young and stupid to plan it all properly. Then, foot-and-mouth hit – and there was just no way we were going to be able to make the shop work. It really was doomed for so many reasons.

Yes, it was always going to be hard work but foot-and-mouth just made it impossible.

It didn't cost us £25,000 – which, I think, the landlord initially wanted – to get out of our lease. The final figure was a lot less than that – but before we ended up doing a deal, we just did a moonlight flit. We turned up with a van, emptied the shop and just went. We thought, 'It's costing us more to open the door than to keep it shut' – so we just decided it wasn't worth us carrying on. And I did think the original shop in Heysham would be OK – if we could just get out of Kendal.

On the bright side, we managed to reuse some of the equipment in the first shop. Also, we could have ended up having to pay off the entire lease – we had signed for it, so that was technically a possibility – and that would have been so much more money lost. I got in touch with the landlord and fortunately he did compromise. He said to me, 'What about all the farmers? They're struggling as well.' I said, 'They're probably getting help – they'll be getting grants from the government, but we're getting nothing.' Anyway, we had a figure we settled on in the end that we paid the landlord – and we had to borrow that money to pay him off. I think it was about £15,000. It could have been a lot worse.

Me and Sue were both so stressed out and there were plenty of arguments between us. I felt so guilty about the situation we were in because it had been more my idea than Sue's idea. She hadn't been as keen as I had been. At the time – even though the whole thing had been more my idea than Sue's – we were probably blaming each other for the mess we were in. There would have been shouting matches between us – and the use of the old silent treatment. But I was probably just a bit more stubborn about everything – the first shop and our marriage. I could never have seen myself walking away from Sue or the business. And thankfully things eventually worked out.

When we expanded the bakery side of the business in 2021, by moving production away from the bakehouse attached to the Heysham shop to bigger premises, what we went through in Kendal all came flooding back – and we said back then we would not be taking on anything that we couldn't afford to pay for.

When we finally got out of it all and left the Kendal shop, it was a feeling of utter relief. It wasn't sadness, just relief. The worst-case scenario was that we would have somehow had to find the money to pay for the rent and rates for the next two years – but even with that scenario, which thankfully didn't actually come to pass, it would still have been a relief to be out of there. It had been £32,000 a year in rent and rates, so it could easily have been £64,000 we had to face paying. To end up losing around £40,000 to £45,000 – well, it could have been a lot worse.

On our many family visits to Kendal we could easily drive past where our shop was, but we never do – we always avoid it. I suppose we've just got to tell ourselves that the positive things are that we became far more cautious about money and learned a lot of lessons.

But what a time – what a terrible time.

Chapter 4

Daniel, Luke, Millie and Katie

Daniel Leon
Born March 3, 1999

Sue: As we said in the previous chapter, life was good in 1999 – we opened our first shop in February, then welcomed our fifth child, Daniel, the following month. We were so happy. Daniel weighed 6lb 6oz, the pregnancy was fine – and the labour was quite funny, although maybe not at the time! I was in a kind of slow labour with Daniel for a few days and then this one day I had a show about 4pm. I called the midwife, who told me I'd better go in.

By the time Noel came home I was having some really strong contractions. So, we got in the car and Noel was saying, 'Oh, I just want to go to Asda to pick up some snacks.' I was like, 'Are you being serious?' And he was saying, 'Yeah, because I don't want to be hungry during the long labour.'

So, I'm there sitting in the car in the car park at Asda, holding onto the head-rest and thinking, 'Where is he? What is he doing? He really should be back by now. Why is he taking this long?' Honestly, he must have been gone for a good half-hour – probably more like 40 minutes. Then he came out, all casual and relaxed, and told me, 'Oh, I just bumped into Tom, the next-door neighbour.' Again, I said, 'Are you being serious? I feel like I'm going to have this baby now. Just get me to the hospital!' But there was no urgency, no rush from Noel what-soever – he was away with the fairies! Daniel was born just an hour after we finally got to the hospital.

Noel: I remember when I was talking to Tom, he asked me, 'How's Sue doing?' And I told him, 'Oh, she's just started her labour – she's in the car.' Tom said, 'Well, you'd better go, then!' I think I was just relaxed at this stage of us being parents – this was going to be our fifth child, after all! And I just thought, I'm going to be there for the long haul so I'd better get ready for it – I needed my snacks and my dinner. I was only doing my prep! I'd never taken snacks in before, so I thought, 'I've learned my lesson here.' But, in the end, because Daniel arrived so soon after we got to the hospital, I had no time to eat them!

Sue: Exactly! What was the point?

Noel: I think it was before Daniel's birth, while we were waiting, that I saw an aeroplane flying past the window – and I was saying to Sue, 'I wonder how long that takes to do a mile.'

Sue: And I was like, 'I'm not interested! I'm having contrac-tions!' Anyway, unlike me when I was waiting for Noel outside Asda and when he was going on about aeroplanes at the hospital,

Daniel was very chilled-out. There was no colic and he wasn't a whingey baby at all.

Noel: Yes, he was really good. Daniel was a very down-to-earth, normal, well-behaved lad – including at school.

Sue: There was some drama, though, when he was about three. I was taking him round to a friend's house. I had to get him out of the car so I could then get his next younger brother, Luke, out of his car seat. So, I first got Daniel out and put him on the pavement and he kind of fell in between the car and the kerb – and he broke his leg! It was one of his shin bones, and he was in plaster for a bit for that.

Noel: But we had no problems with Daniel throughout his schooldays, never a phone call home or anything. He always loved sport – loved football, and he loves it to this day. He doesn't play it much anymore, but he used to play in a local five-a-side team. He was very keen and we ended up taking him to Preston for this trial type thing, when he was about 16.

You had to play in this random five-a-side team, where no one knew each other, and it was being filmed and watched back by the scouts. Nothing ever came of it, and he was quite disappointed about that. After school, he worked for us for a bit – and he's worked at different power stations. He worked at Heysham power station, then he went away to work for a bit at the one in Hartlepool – and he's been to the Hinkley Point one in Somerset, as well.

Sue: Again, like all the kids, he's shown he's not afraid of hard work. They have all been brought up to appreciate the value of hard work.

Luke James
Born October 1, 2000

Sue: Things were still looking rosy when Luke arrived in the world – we had no idea that the shop we would be opening in a couple of months' time would be hit by disaster early the following year. The pregnancy was straightforward, and he was 7lb 6oz. I had been planning on a water birth, and they filled the pool up ready for me to get in it and then they broke my waters. But Luke then pooed inside me – which meant I couldn't have a water birth, and I was absolutely gutted. Because of what happened, I remember they had to suction his mouth.

Noel: Not the best start in life, is it?

Sue: I was a bit gutted because he was my one and only chance to have a water birth. But apart from that dynamic entrance, he was an easy baby, really. He slept through after only about seven or eight weeks.

Noel: He didn't have much hair, did he?

Sue: No, he never had much hair. Luke was really, really placid and got on really well playing with other children – he used to share really well, whereas some of our kids were never up for sharing. Luke was really good like that. And he really liked school. He wasn't really a sporty person. He used to get picked for running and things but he never used to like doing it – it wasn't really his thing.

Noel: I think Luke is the only one who wasn't interested in sport – he still isn't.

Sue: He's more of a computer geek, isn't he? He was just really good at school, though he never went to college or anything like that, even though he has got a keen interest in engineering.

Noel: He worked at McDonald's while he was at school, and I think he stayed there for a little bit after he left school. And he's been working for us in the bakery since then. Engineering is his thing, that's what he wants to get into at some point – and he'll get there eventually.

Sue: We were really, really proud of Luke when he came out as bisexual in such a public way – in front of the cameras on the TV show. I think, as a parent, you just know, he didn't even need to say anything as far as we were concerned – we already knew anyway. But we were really proud of how he handled it – and by doing it on the programme, he has helped other people.

We got a message afterwards from someone who was in their 40s and had never told anyone he was gay, but after watching the programme he did. He told his parents, and he said to us he just wanted to thank Luke for helping him to do that – which was really emotional for us. Luke wasn't bothered about any kind of negativity – he doesn't let anything get to him, ever. So, he was never bothered about doing what he did and he said, 'If I can help other people – or just one person – with how they're feeling, then I want to do that.' Luke is so wise beyond his years. His words are always so wise – if you want some advice about something, you can talk to Luke about it and he'll have some good words for you. He's so articulate.

Noel: I don't think what he did was a big weight off his shoulders. He was probably glad to tell us, but I don't think it was something that really bothered him. And why should it be something that bothers anybody?

Sue: We did have people who messaged us to say, 'I wish my parents had responded like you and Noel did to Luke because I didn't have that with my parents.' But, you know, to us...what does it matter, anyway?

Millie Jo
Born August 29, 2001

Sue: Everything had changed for us by the time Millie was born. It was our year of business hell – and we were forced to bail out of our second shop just a few weeks after celebrating the appearance of Millie, our seventh child. The stress around that Kendal shop was enormous – so thank God for our wonderful children. They kept us going. Millie was 7lb 6oz, exactly the same weight as Luke.

There are only 10 months between Luke and Millie and they were in the same school year growing up – everybody always used to think they were twins. I think they wanted to outdo each other at times – they were rivals. Millie was similar to Luke in some ways. It was difficult, at times, because they were so close together in age – if one started crying it would often start the other one off. So, it was hard at times bringing them up.

Noel: It was almost like having twins at times, wasn't it?

Sue: Yeah. But them going to school in the same school year was always really nice because they each had someone to go to school with. Millie was definitely a drama queen from the very start – very loud!

Noel: We've always said she doesn't talk; she shouts!

Sue: I think that was partly because when she was younger, I remember taking her to this medical appointment and they were looking in her ear and they pulled out this huge clump of earwax. It was massive. But yes, she's always been loud.

Noel: At school, like so many of them, she liked running and was very good at it.

Sue: She was a bit of a nightmare at school, wasn't she? Oh gosh...

Noel: She's always been a handful!

Sue: She was the total opposite to Luke. She was really hard work at school.

Noel: She didn't particularly like school.

Sue: And I don't think they liked her, probably because she was so loud. She wasn't allowed to go to her prom because ...well, her behaviour was not great, was it? And I think that decision has always affected her. The same thing had happened with Sophie.

Noel: I wouldn't say she was naughty.

Sue: No, she was just loud and wanted to have a bit of a laugh and a joke.

Noel: That was her downfall, wasn't it, her mouth? She'd talk when she wasn't supposed to talk and get into trouble for that. But she wasn't one of those kids who would set fire alarms off.

Sue: After leaving school, she did a bit of care work where she would go around to people's houses and help them out.

Noel: First, though, she worked in the shop for us and then had a brief spell at McDonald's. Then she went into the care thing, and then she had the first of her three children, Ophelia.

Katie Louise
Born November 14, 2002

Sue: It had been more than a year since we'd closed the Kendal shop and although it would still be a good while before we got straight financially, things were a good deal less stressful than they had been. It had been such a relief to cut our losses and go back to concentrating on the shop and bakery in Heysham.

Katie was my really fast labour. My waters broke at home just as I was leaving the house, and I remember we were driving to hospital – but Noel hadn't put petrol in the car! We therefore had to stop for petrol while I'm almost pushing this baby out in the front seat! Noel was putting the petrol in and looking at me in the car at the same time, and I'm just thinking, 'You're an absolute idiot, I'm going to end up having this baby here and now.' I moaned at him all the way there and he was driving down the bus lane.

Noel: Yeah, and people were tooting at us!

Sue: Then we got to the hospital and the midwife came out with a wheelchair and the delivery equipment, possibly thinking she's going to have to deliver the baby outside the hospital. She was saying, 'You need to get out' and I was saying, 'I can't move.' I somehow got out and into this wheelchair and within a few minutes of getting in the hospital Katie was born. And as well as being the fastest, she was the heaviest – 9lb 3oz. And she just shot out!

Katie was a good baby but she didn't sleep that brilliantly. In fact, I don't think she slept through until she was about one. But she was a good baby. We've always said Katie is one of our highly-strung children, but she's lovely – she'll do anything for anyone. She loves all her brothers and sisters, she's really good with them. She's always wanted to do childcare, so she's doing that now. She was good at school – and she was really good at running, especially cross country running. She competed for the school and did really well. There are so many in the family who love running and are good at it, and I think it comes from you, Noel. But yes, Katie can be highly-strung. I think sometimes, if Katie is tired, she doesn't tolerate the kids very well.

Noel: She has quite a short fuse!

Sue: If they're annoying her, then she'll just go off on one and say, 'They're doing my head in!'

Noel: The thing is she works with kids all day long – and then comes home to some little ones! If she was coming home to just teenagers, it would probably be a different thing, but when she's worked with toddlers all day it just gets too much for her sometimes. But she is such a caring young woman – that's why she went into that line of work. And she's always saying to us, 'Can I take the kids to the shop with me?' She's always wanting to help out and do things with them – take them out on their bikes and things like that. She's just lovely with them.

Sue: She is so good with kids and she helps us out no end. But it's just that after a tough day at work, she can get a little stressed out with them – which is perfectly understandable because she works so hard.

Chapter 5

Having a vasectomy was the worst thing I ever did – getting it reversed was the best

Noel: I think I should put things in context here – give you some perspective. It was June 2003. Our most recent child, Katie, had been our eighth – and Sue was pregnant with our ninth (and we'll be hearing about James – and others – in the next chapter). That, we accept, is a lot of children – several more than will be in the average family. But to remind you of our ages that summer, when I underwent my vasectomy, I was 32 and Sue just 28.

Maybe it was the number of kids we had rather than our ages that had been on people's minds for so long. I think the peer pressure we faced for me to get a vasectomy – little comments from family and friends – probably started after we had Daniel, our fifth child. And it just progressed from there, really. It came from inside and outside the family – but it was never nasty, or anything like that.

Sue: It was just comments like, 'Oh, do you think you're going to get the snip now?' and, 'Do you think you've got enough kids?' – things like that. Like Noel says, there was nothing malicious – and people all over the country must make those kinds of comments to parents who have had a few kids. It wouldn't have been something that we weren't expecting to happen.

Noel: It was all jokey and lighthearted and at first, you're just thinking to yourself, 'Yeah, stuff you – I'm not interested!' But, then, the longer it went on, I suppose it did get under our skin a little bit, and you're bound to start thinking more about it because so many people have been talking about how I should maybe get a vasectomy.

I can't really remember how the discussions between me and Sue about having it done actually started. But I don't think we did have those conversations before Sue was pregnant with James – our ninth child. So, you can imagine, if the comments began after we'd had Daniel, our fifth, they obviously went on for a good while – and must have really got into our heads. Daniel was born in March 1999, and we would have found out Sue was pregnant with James early in 2003 because he was born in the October of that year – so that's a good few years of people asking, 'Are you going to have the snip now?'

Sue: I'm struggling to remember how it all happened, too. I think it was when we announced we were expecting James – and it was all, 'Oh, you'll really need to get the snip sorted out now.' In the end, the time between having the actual appointment about having the vasectomy to having it done was only about six weeks – which is not a long time, when you think of how big a decision it is to make.

Noel: Looking back, it was probably a case of me and Sue not talking to each other about how we really felt. If we had been open with each other and had a really good talk about it all, we would have concluded that we didn't want to do it.

Sue: That's right, but I think we somehow found ourselves in a position where we were just saying to each other, after all the pressure we'd been under, 'Yeah, let's just get it done. It would stop people moaning and keep them happy.'

Noel: That really was it – it was more a case of shutting them up, rather than properly thinking about what we wanted.

Sue: I think we gave into the pressure and, because you love your family and your friends, you just want to please them. I don't think we thought about ourselves as much as we should have done. We got swept along with it all, because there were so many people all saying the same thing – and they had been saying it for an awfully long time.

Noel: The same sort of thing must happen in so many other families. I think it starts out as a bit of a joke, maybe after you've had two kids – and then the more you have the more it builds up, and the comments then probably get a bit more serious. And it also might have been in the back of our minds that we had a really bad year – in 2001 – just two years before we made this decision. There had been so much stress after we had taken on that second shop in Kendal and we ended up losing so much money. I can't remember if that was part of our discussions – 'What if something similar happened again?' – but it could possibly have been a factor in our thinking.

I think it was more the pressure that had built up after all the comments that had been made. It seems mad now, but in the days leading up to the vasectomy – and on the day itself – I was thinking, 'I don't want to do this.' But, somehow, I felt I was too far down the line. In my mind, there seemed to be no going back. Then it was, like, 'We're here now at the hospital, let's just get it done.' But, of course, when you look back and think about it, it really shouldn't have been like that.

Sue: What I always find really, really odd – because I've heard other stories about this since – is that there wasn't any kind of counselling back then after you'd asked about having a vasectomy. Now, if you want to have a hysterectomy or a vasectomy, you've got to go for counselling to make sure you're both 100% on the same page and you want to have it done. But there was nothing like that back then.

I feel that if there had been that counselling in place then we wouldn't have been in the situation of Noel ending up having it done. It would have all been talked through with us and we would have come to the conclusion that it really wasn't something we wanted. I think they're quite strict now on having counselling sessions, but we just never had that opportunity.

Noel: It wasn't as if I was taken into a quiet room on the day, and asked, 'Do you really want to do this? Are you totally sure?' There was nothing like that. There was myself and probably four or five other guys there having it done – and you were just called in when it was your turn and you had the procedure.

You think about the ages we were – me 32, and Sue 28 – and how many more kids we may have wanted in the future and how many we could have actually had if we decided not to go ahead with the vasectomy. But we weren't asked about anything like that. It's horrible to say, but they could also have asked, 'What happens if you separate? You're both still young – what if you end up wanting a family with someone else?'

Sue: Nowadays, especially if you're quite young, I think it's very difficult to get it done. There's certainly counselling involved, with discussions taking place about how you might feel in the future.

Noel: Yeah, that just never happened with us, which is probably why it all went ahead. And I don't think any man who has had the snip will forget the procedure – not least because you're awake when it happens. It was all pretty quick, maybe 20 minutes or less, and pretty straightforward – they just said you might feel a bit of tugging and movement, and that was it. I don't recall any problems afterwards – I wasn't walking like John Wayne or anything. And there wasn't any pain. Sue drove me home very soon after the vasectomy, and the regrets about having it done were there immediately – straight after coming out of the hospital.

Sue: I don't think me and Noel were getting on too great at the time – probably starting from when the appointment had been made six weeks before the vasectomy was carried out. It was the realisation that it was all final and that there would be no more children – our relationship definitely changed at that time.

Noel: We definitely fell out over it.

Sue: At the time, I was probably thinking it was because of business-related stress, and because I was pregnant with James – but now I think it was all because of the vasectomy.

Noel: It was crazy because, deep down, neither of us wanted it to happen. Somehow, it seemed to be a case of, 'It's going to be done and that's all there is to it. Nothing can change the path we're on.'

Sue: It was probably a case of us just not talking enough, with me thinking to myself, 'Why is he having this done?' and Noel thinking, 'Why won't Sue tell me she doesn't think I should have it done?'

Noel: Our mood was very low, but I think it was within a few days that we started looking into whether we could have the vasectomy reversed. Sue found out that I could – and that the sooner we got it done the better, because there was a greater chance of it being successful if it was done within two years of the vasectomy being carried out.

It took a while, but we got it sorted out – and, this time, we were both 100% about it from the outset. I never had any doubts about going ahead with the reversal. I knew it was a bigger and more complicated procedure than the vasectomy, but I always wanted to go ahead with it – from the minute we had arranged it to the minute I was put under so they could carry it out. We knew this was what we definitely wanted – and it was the best thing I ever did. The vasectomy had been a terrible mistake, and was the worst thing I ever did.

Sue: We had to save up for the reversal procedure for several months, because you can't have it done on the NHS.

Noel: I think it was about £1,300. But it was obviously worth every penny. And although it is a more complicated procedure than having a vasectomy, I don't remember having any pain afterwards – although I was given strong painkillers. I just recall the multi-coloured bruises.

Sue: Noel, it was literally all black!

Noel: The whole of it – the veg as well as the meat!

Sue: Honestly, I have never, ever seen anything like it.

Noel: I remember looking at it and thinking, 'That's never going to get better!'

Sue: But apparently, they did warn you it would look a lot worse than after the vasectomy.

Noel: They said there would be SOME bruising. They didn't tell me how extreme it would be! Sue, you really must stop laughing! Anyway, not surprisingly, it was a fair few weeks before it all cleared up and I was back to normal. But for a while, I was thinking, 'Maybe there was no point having the vasectomy reversed, because I won't be able to use it again!'

Sue: That's so funny! And looking back, Noel, I must admit, after everything I had been through during so many pregnancies, I did kind of feel, 'It's good to see Noel suffering for a change! Now he knows just a little bit about how it's been for me.' Then again, he wasn't even in any pain with it all, because of the strong painkillers he was on! But it was still a bit of pay-back time to an extent – especially when you think about how he looked down there!

Noel: At least the kids didn't laugh at me – though that's probably because we never told them! I went to the hospital in the morning – I think you must have told them I was at some kind of business meeting all day, Sue, and then you had to come out at night time to pick me up and bring me home. Then I walked through the door – or tried to walk as best as I could! – and pretended I'd just been in this meeting all day.

I had to be careful with all these lively kids around, because I was so tender – there was no, 'Come and have a cuddle with Dad' for a little while, it was a case of, 'Just sit on the chair next to me.' All these years on, none of the older kids have really talked to me about it all – and the fact that they might not have had their younger brothers and sisters. And the younger ones – the ones who came after the reversal – haven't really talked to me about it either.

I don't suppose it's the kind of thing you talk to your dad about – 'If you hadn't had your nuts repaired, I wouldn't be here!' Maybe it will happen over a drink in the pub at some point in the future!

Sue: I do quite often think, Noel, 'If you didn't have the vasectomy reversed, there would have been no kids from Ellie onwards' – and that's just amazing. It's really hard to get your head around that. We've had more kids since the reversal than we had before it. It's just incredible to think that is the case. I'd actually got pregnant with Ellie – who was born in May 2005 – within two months of the reversal being done.

Noel: Once we had saved up and I had eventually been able to arrange an appointment – one doctor refused to put me forward because I'm guessing I hadn't been convincing enough about wanting to have it done – the reversal was carried out by a brilliant man called Dr Richard Wilson. Sadly, Dr Wilson has passed away, but it was lovely to be able to meet his son, Murray, for the TV series. As we told him, we owe his dad so much.

Sue: Our family and friends – all the people who had been suggesting Noel had a vasectomy for all those years – couldn't say anything about any of this, because we didn't tell them! I remember, later, just after I got pregnant with Ellie – our 10th child – I had the midwife round to the house. I knew my mum and dad were coming round on that day, but I thought they'd arrive a little bit later. But they turned up while the midwife was there, so that's how they found out that we hadn't stopped at nine children! I think they were looking at me and wondering, 'How has this happened?' But we never told anyone at that stage about the reversal.

Noel: I think we did say, at one point, that the vasectomy can't have worked.

Sue: We didn't actually come clean and tell people about the reversal until the summer of 2015 – after we'd had our 18th child, Hallie!

Noel: Nobody had ever said to us what they thought must have happened. It was just never discussed. But what I will never forget are our reactions when we found out Sue was pregnant with Ellie, not long after I'd had the reversal. It was a case of, 'Thank God it worked!' We were just overjoyed – absolutely over the moon. We did fear that maybe it wouldn't work and we wouldn't be able to have any more children, so it was a mix of joy and relief.

Sue: I simply couldn't believe it. I was so happy. But I think we were both quite shocked – shocked that it had happened so quickly after the reversal.

Noel: I think from the day of the reversal being carried out, things got better between me and Sue. We had both really wanted the reversal to happen and everything changed that day. We couldn't know for sure that it would work and that Sue would have more children, but we knew this was what we wanted to happen – that we had to give ourselves a chance to have more children. I remember ringing you up from my hospital bed, Sue, and telling you, 'I've had it done!' I was still half asleep with all the drugs they must have given me, but I remember you were cheering down the phone!

Sue: You look back now, after all these years, to that decision that was made for Noel to have a vasectomy – and it was a decision that could have torn us apart as a couple and as a family. We really weren't getting on well around that whole period. But we just didn't have that counselling that really should have been available for people in our situation – we were still so young.

Noel: If anyone ever came to me to ask for my advice – because they were thinking about having a vasectomy – I'd just tell them,

'Please, take your time, because this could be a one-way ticket. You've got to REALLY think about it.'

Sue: It was a really happy ending for us – but we know that might not have been the case.

Noel: We're just so grateful that the reversal worked, and that we were able to go on and have so many more kids. We made a big mistake, but you're right, Sue, it was a happy ending.

Chapter 6

James, Ellie, Aimee and Josh

James Edward
Born October 17, 2003

Sue: This was such a strange time for me and Noel as parents – we were so delighted with the arrival of James, and yet Noel had undergone his vasectomy and we were saving up so he could have it reversed. Though, of course, at this stage, we had no idea if the reversal would be successful. I did suffer from postnatal depression after having James – linked, I'm sure, to Noel's vasectomy, and I'll talk about this in more detail later in the book.

James was my first one who was induced after Katie – and this became a common occurrence, in response to Katie having been such a quick labour. He was around a five-hour labour after the breaking of my waters, and was 8lb 2oz. James was quite an easy baby, apart from the fact he didn't really sleep very well – he was more than one by the time he started sleeping through regularly. But he was always – and he still is now – quite a comedian. He's always smiling and happy – a real joker.

Noel: But he was quite studious at school. He went, kept his head down and got on with his work. He was no trouble at all. But, unlike most of the other kids, he wasn't overly sporty.

Sue: No, he was a bit like Luke, really. He never really liked sport.

Noel: With him being a comedian and always looking for laughs, he would try and push the boundaries a bit at home.

Sue: He was quite close to Katie, and when Josh came along, after Ellie and Aimee, the two lads became really close – and they still are now.

Noel: With James being in between girls – Katie and Ellie – he was in a bit of a pickle for a time...kind of, 'I've got sisters to hang around with, all my brothers are a bit older, so it's not the same.'

Sue: So, when Josh came along, nearly four years later, he had his playmate at last.

Noel: James did some weird stuff when he was younger. He used to stick window putty and bits of paper up his nose! We never knew at the time – it was properly stuffed up there – but what we eventually noticed was this bad smell. It was like meat that had gone off, it was really disgusting.

We took him to the doctor and he told us he'd got stuff stuck up his nose, but he couldn't get to it. It gets worse, because Sue had to blow in his mouth to make it come out of his nose.

Oh, that smell – God knows how long the putty had been up there. But it never seemed to bother James!

Sue: Oh God, I remember them making me do that and it was awful – absolutely disgusting. He was about three at the time. I remember the nursery teacher saying there just seemed to be a bit of a bad smell coming from his nose. He later stuck something else up his nose – I can't remember what – but we managed to get that out straight away. But, thank God, James calmed down the older he got and stopped doing that sort of thing!

Noel: After school, he went to college to do forensic science and he did about a year of that. But it wasn't really what he was expecting, so he left. Then he got a girlfriend in Blackpool and went to live there, getting a job at the Fisherman's Friend factory in nearby Fleetwood. Then there was a parting of the ways, so he came back home and he's had a few jobs since then – one was at a giant launderette, and now he's at a place where they make moulds; he'd be in his element if they involved putty!

Ellie May
Born May 6, 2005

Sue: Ah, as we explained in the last chapter, we were absolutely over the moon when we discovered I was pregnant with Ellie. The vasectomy reversal had worked! The joy and the relief we felt were just incredible – off the scale!

Noel: It was a very emotional time. We had really been through it with the vasectomy. But thank God I was able to get the reversal done, and thank God it worked. We felt very blessed and very fortunate. We were going to have our 10th child – and maybe there would be more to follow!

Sue: Ellie was induced, about a three-hour labour and weighed 7lb 6oz. She was a really good baby – there were no issues with her at all. She must have slept through from about three months. And she was really good at school – there were never any problems with Ellie. She was very sporty, and she still loves her sport. She's now doing sport at college.

Noel: She goes to the gym a couple of times a week and was very good at cross country at school. The running side was the main thing for her.

Sue: Bless her, whenever Ellie used to get upset when she was younger, she used to cry and go all red and blotchy in her face. It was really bad and we were always like, 'Oh Ellie, please stop crying' – and we'd go and get her some sweets to stop her from crying.

Noel: She was very clever – she knew how to get us to give her sweets!

Sue: It was in 2022 that Ellie was diagnosed with Gilbert's syndrome (where slightly higher than normal levels of a substance called bilirubin build up in the blood, which can lead to a yellowing of the skin and the whites of the eyes – jaundice). At the time, she was doing her exams and under a lot of stress because of that as she was working really hard. We'd been on holiday to Florida, and I remember coming home and thinking, 'She's lost so much weight in just a week.' She was really tired and said she had bad pains in her stomach. Then she said she had pain in the top of her legs.

One of our friends – her daughter is going through cancer treatment – said to me, 'I don't mean to worry you, but she's at the right age for getting leukaemia.' I was thinking, 'Oh my God.' We went to the doctor that day and got her bloods checked.

She called the next day and told me Ellie's bilirubin levels were up – I didn't know what that was and was immediately worried, but the doctor told me it could be something called Gilbert's syndrome, and she explained that it wasn't serious but at times of great stress the levels of bilirubin in her liver might go really high and make her feel poorly. Now we just need to make sure Ellie avoids stressful situations – but there's no medication needed.

It's apparently really common and a lot of people won't know they have it, because they deal with stress in a different way. Ellie wants to end up doing something involving sport. She's hoping to be something like a personal trainer.

Aimee Elizabeth
Born April 21, 2006

Sue: No, we didn't hang around after the good news that Noel's vasectomy reversal had worked. Ellie had arrived in May 2005, and here was Aimee – born the following April! I think you can probably work out that, having been given our second chance after the reversal, we weren't hanging about adding to our beautiful family.

Aimee was also induced, and was about a four-hour labour. She was 7lb 2oz, and was a really good baby. It was so lovely that there wasn't much of an age difference between Aimee and Ellie, because it led to them being really close when they were growing up – while they still are today. There were never any issues with Aimee at school, she always did really well. Like Ellie, she really enjoyed school.

Noel: Aimee was another good cross country runner – maybe not as keen as some of the others, but she was definitely good at it when she did it. But she was more academic, and enjoyed doing all her coursework.

With some of them, they need a bit of encouragement to do their homework, but Aimee was never like that. She just got on with it. And she never got up to anything daft – like sticking putty up her nose! She was, and remains, lovely – she has never given us any problems. Aimee likes her music, and is another Taylor Swift fan – like her mum and some of the other older girls.

Sue: Aimee works in our shop at the moment but after school she started doing hairdressing at college – and now she's qualified to do my hair! I think she'll probably end up doing everyone's hair in the house – she'll never be short of customers here!

Noel: They'll all be wanting it done for free, though, that's the only problem. Poor Aimee – she'll have to watch herself there! She's been a great worker in the shop but we know hairdressing is what she eventually wants to do full-time.

Josh Benjamin
Born July 3, 2007

Noel: There were no problems with Josh as a baby and it wasn't long before he was sleeping through.

Sue: He was also induced, about a two-hour labour and weighed 8lb 6oz when he was born. And yeah, he was a good baby – and there are plenty of stories about what he got up to when he was very young!

Noel: He did have a tendency to relieve himself in swimming pools – and unfortunately, we're not talking about peeing in the pool, as so many kids have done! The first time, we were in France – Josh must have been three – and it was like one of these splash parks; the water was only about a foot deep at the most. I looked down at the water and there was this big, brown cloud around him!

I just thought, 'What are we going to do here?' It was really busy, full of French people, and I thought, 'I haven't a clue what I'm going to say if someone comes up to me about it.' We got him out, dealt with him and then turned around and saw that all the brown had gone – the chemicals must have eaten it all up.

Sue: But a couple of weeks later, we were in Lanzarote with my mum and dad – and it happened again. We'd gone to get dinner with some of the other kids and my mum and dad were left with Josh and, I think, Aimee and Ellie. Josh did it again in the pool and my mum had to deal with it – it was everywhere, the pool was just brown.

There was this other guy we got friendly with and he could speak a little bit of Spanish, but he didn't know how to say, 'He's had a poo in the pool' in Spanish, so he just went up to the lifeguard and said, 'He's had a shit in the pool!'

Noel: This time it didn't quite disperse in the same way, unfortunately.

Sue: When we got back from having our dinner, my mum was like, 'Don't ever leave me with him again! He's had a poo in the pool and they've had to put all these chemicals in it.' Oh my God, it was terrible.

Noel: By this stage, no one was in the pool because they'd said, 'Give it half an hour for the chemicals to start working' – and I remember this posh lady came up and said to her friend, 'Oh look, the pool is nice and quiet. Let's go in!' And in they went!

Sue: When you ask Josh about it now, he says, 'I remember that, but I didn't want to go to the toilet because it had spiders in it.'

Noel: Josh is just an absolute class clown – he is so funny. Ellie recently reminded us about the time we went to Florida a few years ago and Josh went ironing board surfing – and it all went wrong.

Sue: He was very lucky – watching the video of it – that he didn't break his neck. He's so bad, isn't he? But he's just not bothered.

Noel: He's great entertainment at home, though – so funny to be around.

Sue: I think that's one of the reasons why things didn't go so well for him at school.

Noel: Yes, let's just say Josh wasn't quite as academic as some of the others.

Sue: He just always wanted to have a laugh and a joke – but you can't do that at school, can you? He was forever getting in trouble. The school decided it would be better for him to go to college a year early to do sport, which was absolutely amazing for him. He became a totally different person.

They'd said to us, 'We don't do this lightly because it costs the school an awful lot of money to send anyone to college a year early, but we really think it could benefit Josh.' And wow, it was amazing for him – he loved it and thrived.

Noel: Some kids just don't fit in at school and it's not for them. It was the same with Chris and Millie – school was never their thing, either. I think Josh wants to end up doing something sporty, but also to get a trade of some kind.

Chapter 7

Max, Tillie, Oscar and Casper

Max Joseph
Born December 11, 2008

Sue: Yes, we were still very much on a roll, after Noel's vasectomy reversal – and why not? We had been so down when we thought we wouldn't be able to have any more children. Me and Noel just loved having kids, and we were so grateful for our second chance.

There was nothing unlucky about Max, our 13th. He was kind of a Christmas baby for us – born just two weeks before what is always a really special day for our family. And, of course, he was our baker's dozen!

Noel: Not only that, but because his birth had the ingredients of a good newspaper story – in the view of our local paper in

Morecambe, *The Visitor* – we found ourselves being put in the media spotlight for the first time. They loved the fact that I was a baker and Max was our 13th child. The story was also followed up by the *Lancashire Evening Post*. Fame at last – though it would be a few more years before television got involved.

Sue: Max was induced, and weighed 8lb 8oz. But although he was a good baby, Max was so difficult to feed because he kind of put his tongue up to the top of his mouth and his jaw was set back as well. It just made feeding him an absolute nightmare. He only breast-fed for about a week and then we had to change to bottles because he was losing too much weight.

He did sleep through from about six months, but from very early on we knew there was something a bit different with him. He would get toys – cars and things – and he would line them all up in colour order. Max would just do things differently and we wondered if he maybe had autism. In primary school, there really started to be problems in Year Four, when he was eight. He wanted to run out of school when things weren't going his way.

Noel: He'd hide from certain teachers – in the middle of all the PE equipment in the hall – and they'd say, 'Come on Max, you need to come out.' And he'd reply, 'I can see you, but you can't see me.' Then he'd say, 'I'm going to run out of the school' and he'd just go and hide in a bush somewhere. But at that time, one of the teachers – she was bloody awful, Miss Trunchbull we called her (after the fictional headmistress of Crunchem Hall Primary School in the film *Matilda*).

She had no patience with kids like Max, and got us in to tell us, 'If he doesn't improve, he's going to be suspended.' I was thinking 'Flipping hell, he's in Year Four – and it's not as if he's throwing things at teachers or kicking them or anything

– and she's talking about suspending him.' Luckily, the Year Six teacher, who had been there forever, said, 'If he does it again, I'm supposed to report it, but I'm not going to because I think there's something wrong here.' And he got someone else involved and eventually Max was assessed and they said he was on the autism spectrum.

Sue: It was so difficult to get tested back then. You had to go on a waiting list and it just took forever. I can remember thinking that he was never going to get diagnosed until he got to high school, and that we were not going to get any help for him. But, thankfully, we did and they were then really, really good at his school. When he wanted to hide, they organised a special area where he could go and sit and calm down a little bit before he was ready to go back. And it worked. When he went to high school, we were worried he wouldn't be able to cope in a big, mainstream school but he's thrived.

Noel: He loves Maths, Science, and studying the universe and nature.

Sue: He is so, so bright – he can tell you things which you have absolutely no clue about.

Noel: Looking back, I think that's where Josh's problems started at school – because that same teacher gave him a lot of hassle. Josh was in the football team for the primary school and they won their way to play in the final at Wembley.

This teacher said, 'We've got a new rule, three strikes and then there'll be consequences.' Well, he had two – for nothing; he hadn't done his homework, or something like that. Then he was playing football with his friends in the designated area in the playground and these girls kept coming in their way, to annoy them, and Josh kicked the ball which hit this girl in the face and she went running off to the teachers.

Sure enough, he was banned from going to Wembley. So, this was Year Six – which meant Josh ended up missing out on playing at Wembley when he was just 10. It still bothers Josh to this day and will affect him for the rest of his life. Morecambe FC were involved in it as well, and the woman there was very good. She said, 'I can still arrange for him to go, though he won't be able to play. But at half-time, at least, he could have a kickaround with a ball on the pitch.' Josh said, 'No, I'm not doing that.' I sometimes think – because we also had two of the girls not being allowed to go to their proms – that it's a case of teachers thinking, 'It's the Radfords' and having it in for us.'

Sue: But yes, Max is flourishing now – and we're so relieved because we had a lot of sleepless nights, especially around the time of his move from primary school to high school. We'd probably known about his autism from when he was very young – his speech was delayed, and he didn't really start talking until he was about four, which is very late.

I can always remember talking to the health visitor about it, but she would tell me children are all very different – which, yes, they are, but you know your own child and we just knew something wasn't quite right. But then when he did start talking, it all came out at once. He became such a good talker – and wouldn't shut up! And I'm sure now he's looking ahead and wants to do something which involves science.

Noel: I think he would love to work at NASA – that would be his dream. He said he wanted to invent a car that runs on water, but he discovered someone had already done that.

Sue: Honestly, he is so lovely. He has such a good nature.

Noel: There's not a bad bone in his body at all.

Tillie May
Born May 2, 2010

Sue: You might have noticed Tillie has the same middle name as Ellie – because they were both born in May.

Tillie was an amazing baby and slept right through from just three days old. Incredible! She weighed 6lb 3oz. I remember telling the midwife she'd slept right through early on, and she said, 'Oh, you need to wake her up' – I thought, 'Not a chance!' She's been our only baby to have done that. And no colic, no nothing – a dream baby! But later, Tillie began to have a real tough time of it.

When she was 18 months old, she had a prolonged febrile convulsion and nearly died from it. We got her to Royal Lancaster Infirmary but they couldn't get any lines in her because her body was just completely shut down. I remember getting taken out of the room because they said they were going to have to drill into a bone to put a line in, that it was a very last resort and it would not be nice for us to see.

We sat in the waiting room while they put this line in her leg. So, they did that and she was on a ventilator in intensive care for about 10 days. It turned out she had bronchitis and that's what caused the prolonged febrile convulsion. Bear in mind, she had been absolutely fine before that – there had been nothing wrong with her at all.

I remember we'd done the bath routine with the kids one night, and were just sitting on the bed with Tillie watching *In The Night Garden* with her. We'd probably been about 20 minutes late putting the younger kids to bed, but if we hadn't been – if we'd put Tillie to bed at her normal bed time – she probably wouldn't be here today. She came out of intensive care after 10 days and came home. She'd been walking, because she was 18 months old, but suddenly she wouldn't put any pressure on her right leg, where they had drilled into a bone, and it turned out she had got a very slight infection in the site where they had drilled. But they said it was fine and the infection would go away without the need for treatment.

Then it took her about four months to start walking properly again – and fast forward three years or so, and she was standing in front of me in her school uniform and I thought, 'Oh my God, what's going on with her leg?' This bone was sticking out of the side of her leg. We took her to the doctors and they were saying, 'This is definitely not right – we'll send her for an x-ray.' We were then transferred to Alder Hey Children's Hospital in Liverpool and told that when the procedure to drill into her leg was carried out, the infection that came from that damaged the plate in her leg and stopped one of the bones from growing – while the one that was sticking out WAS still growing. She's since had lots of operations to try to lengthen her shorter leg and she's still going through treatment now.

Noel: A couple of years ago, she had this external frame put on her leg, while there were more complications when she shot up in height after hitting puberty. There is still a few centimetres difference in the size of each leg, and, at the time of writing, she's due to have another operation around Spring 2024. The frame will be placed internally this time, rather than externally. She'd been such an outdoors person, as well – she loved being outside and running around. But all the problems with her leg scuppered her straight away, really.

Sue: But Tillie is absolutely amazing, because she just gets on with it. She doesn't let things hold her back. Mentally, though, it was really hard for her when she had that frame on her leg and, at first, she got quite depressed about it. But she wants this next operation to be done, and she's glad that, this time, the frame is going to be on the inside. Tillie's obviously been limited with what she's been able to do, because of the pain she suffers with her leg. She hates sport for that reason, but loves drawing and reading. She likes music, as well. She's doing well at school, but she's quite conscious of her leg – she doesn't like wearing skirts or shorts; she'll wear trousers, instead.

Noel: On holiday, she's fine with it – but if you go walking around the playground, you don't want kids pointing and saying, 'What's that?' Tillie also loves singing – she's always got music on at full blast and will sing along to it. She's still a very confident girl and doesn't let things get her down. We're just obviously looking forward to this next operation – where they will lengthen the leg again, get it the same length as the left leg, and then she'll be fine. But because of everything she's been through, she might end up an inch smaller than she might have been had none of this happened. But we're all vertically challenged in this house, anyway!

Sue: We always say at the end of the day if they hadn't drilled into her leg we could have lost her, and so this is really a small price to pay for her still being here.

Oscar Will
Born October 22, 2011

Sue: Oscar, who was 8lb 8oz, was a really good baby – no problems at all. He probably didn't sleep through until about 10 months or so but, luckily, he started doing so around the time Casper was born – because I remember thinking, 'Oh crikey, I'm going to have to be up with both of them.' He's a lovely lad, Oscar. He's very bright and loves Maths and Science. He's excelled at school, and was reading fluently in Year One – the only one of our children who has been like that.

Noel: Yeah, he's been very advanced for his age all the way through school so far. He's very wise as well. He loves to learn at school – and, probably, he's been the cleverest of all our children.

Sue: He's so bubbly – he's always smiling and making jokes. He won quite a few awards at primary school and he was really excited about going to secondary school, because he just loves learning.

Noel: But he's not really looking ahead and saying he wants to do this or that, involving Maths or Science or whatever, when he leaves school. If anything, he's just a typical lad in this respect – he loves football, and wants to be a footballer! But we wouldn't be surprised if he did end up doing something which involved Maths or Science.

Casper Theo
Born October 3, 2012

Sue: Casper was a straightforward labour, and he was 7lb 6oz. I did find Oscar and Casper really hard work as babies, because there was less than a year between them. That was quite challenging, because if Oscar started crying then he would set Casper off – so it was hard. Do you remember that, Noel?

Noel: Yeah, they were a bit like Luke and Millie.

Sue: Casper was similar to Oscar in that he started to sleep through after about 10 months, so that was good. And although they would set each other off when they did cry, they weren't whingey babies – they were good. Casper, like Oscar, was soon showing that he loved football – he's absolutely obsessed with it. And he's a bit similar to Oscar at school in that he also loves his Maths. He's won quite a few awards at school, too. But he really loves sport – that's his big thing, really.

Noel: Casper's definitely the more sporty out of the two of them. Whereas Oscar will like to play on his Xbox, Casper will be outside with his football – working on all his moves. He's quite a sensitive lad. He can get upset over things – for example, if someone says something he doesn't like.

Sue: Yes, he does, he is very sensitive – but the great thing is that he and Oscar are just inseparable and are such great mates as well as brothers. I remember a teacher saying to me at their primary school – before Oscar left for secondary school – 'Ah, it was so sweet, when Casper was coming out of school the other day he went up to Oscar and gave him a big hug. I can just tell the bond they have is so strong.'

That was lovely to hear and I said, 'Yeah, that's exactly what they're like at home as well. They're best friends.' It's lovely that they are like that and not fighting and bickering, like a lot of brothers are – especially those who are quite close in age. It's just wonderful – but the sad thing, because they are so close and have such a strong bond, was that Casper found it hard when Oscar went off to high school first.

Noel: I remember, not so long ago, we went away for a weekend to Coniston in the Lake District, and Oscar didn't want to come. He wanted to stay at home for some reason, so he stayed with Chris and some of the other older ones – and

Casper didn't realise this was happening until we were setting off. He then asked, 'Is Oscar not coming?' We explained he was staying with Chris, and Casper said to us, 'Well how will I get to sleep if he's not with me?'

Sue: They just love each other so much, and I'm sure that bond will continue into adult life because they will have all those shared experiences from being so close as children.

Chapter 8

We're on the telly!

Sue: I suppose you could say 2012 was the year when our lives really began to change, because it was the year when our TV adventure started.

 Noel: We mentioned earlier about appearing in Morecambe's *Visitor* newspaper and the *Lancashire Evening Post* at the end of 2008. I think it was about a year or two later that a TV production company got in touch. They said, 'We're making a television programme for Channel 4 on big families and we'd like you to be one of them.' We said, 'No, we're not interested.' Because we'd seen these reality shows in the past – things like Benefits Street – and we saw how people came across on them and thought, 'No, we're not being associated with something like that.'

 They pestered us for a couple of months, even though we kept saying 'No.' Then they explained it in a bit more detail, saying it was going to be a positive programme, showing how these big families lived day to day, and then we relented. And we've never looked back since then!

Sue: It was at the start of 2012 – January 17 – that we first appeared on TV, along with several other larger-than-life families. I was actually pregnant with Oscar, our 15th child, when filming for the *15 Kids and Counting* series began, so I suppose it could have been called *14 Kids and Counting*. Although Oscar was born three months before the series was broadcast, viewers initially saw him in my tummy. 2012 really was an incredible, whirlwind year – not least because Casper, our 16th child, arrived in October, and our first grandchild, Daisy, was born in August. We had our Sophie to thank for that – and you'll be able to read about our wonderful grandchildren later in the book.

Noel: Yes, what a year! Looking back on our TV debut, we had no way of knowing what the programme would lead to, if anything. Afterwards, they asked us if we would stay on and do another programme. We were happy to do so, and did another three on our own, with no other families involved. They were single, one-hour shows – and then the production company we were with were getting as frustrated as we were, wondering why they wouldn't do a series instead. They were pushing Channel 4 on this, but they came back and said, 'If you just do one more hour, then we will think about a series' – and we just said, 'No, we're not doing it.'

We put our foot down, basically. And that seemed to be that. Then, eventually, Channel 5 came along – the production company must have spoken to them – and they were pretty much straight away talking about a series. They began by commissioning a four-part series, which was shown in 2021 and was a success – so they then commissioned an eight-part series.

Sue: But then they came back to us saying they actually wanted 10 episodes. And now we're up to 12 – so it's done really well.

Noel: After those initial doubts we had after first hearing about the interest in making a programme about us, it was after watching the very first show that any lingering reservations we may have had disappeared. I think when you're doing your first one, you're in a situation of not knowing how TV works, what they're setting you up for or anything like that. I guess, after it was screened, we became more confident about making the next one – and then since moving over to Channel 5, we've been even happier.

Sue: We love making the show with the team at Lion Television and Channel 5 – we all share the same goal to just show everyday family life for what it really is. No agenda or angle. But I do think people watching must assume it's really easy for us, when it's actually hard work. And, of course, it's intrusive as well, because you're inviting a camera crew into your home and your lives. But we have a really lovely relationship with our camera crew. We've been with the same people for a few years now and we get on really well with them. And it's brilliant because the kids get on really well with them, too.

Noel: It is hard work, not least because it can mess up your daily routine at times. If we are filming all day, for example, then it can mess up basic things which keep the house running day-to-day – like the laundry. It can put you a day behind. But we do find that if they are filming all day, it's not with me all day or with Sue all day – you do get a break, so it's just a matter of trying to arrange things so you can still do all the things you have to do while doing the filming that needs to be done as well.

Sue: I think the best thing about making the programmes is the memories we get to keep forever on film. Because looking back at the shows we've filmed over the years we can see how the kids have changed. It's lovely to have all those memories to look back on in the form of these well-made programmes.

Noel: That's one of the reasons we have said we will keep doing it. And we've said as long as the kids are enjoying it then we'll keep going – if they ever lose interest, that's when it will stop. The thing I least enjoy is probably the fact that I can have just finished a busy day at work and then I come home and go straight into filming – there's no chance to have a break or put your feet up.

It's not as if they're cracking the whip, but they obviously have to get certain things done and it's just that you may already have had a full-on day. But they totally understand if they run out of time to do something – they'll just say, 'Don't worry, we'll get it done another day.' And the way the programmes are made is a bit of a mix – we'll have a meeting at the beginning of the series where we'll say what we have planned for the coming year, and then they will try to work some stories out around that, but we're very late planners so a lot of it will be developed as we go along. We'll say, 'Oh, we were going to do this next week' – and then a story might come from that which they think would be good to film.

Sue: We've made so many episodes over the years, but I've got to say I still hate seeing myself on screen.

Noel: It's your voice you don't like, isn't it?

Sue: Yeah, it is! And it hasn't changed over the years. I just can't get used to seeing and hearing myself. I've never felt comfortable about it. I think it's a normal thing – even some actors say they don't like watching themselves. I do join the others and watch it when it comes on but I'm still kind of, 'Oh no, this is really hard to sit and watch.'

Noel: I don't have the same issues. I'll happily sit and watch it – and quite often you'll go in the living room and the kids are watching it on catch-up or whatever, so they obviously like it, too. There's no escape for Sue – the kids might be playing it at any time! I remember years ago, when we were first on, you'd be getting all excited about it and telling all your friends – now, it's just 'Whatever.' We're glad we're doing it and we enjoy doing it, but we've got used to making the programme now so it's bound to be different from when you gather round as a family to watch it the very first time.

Sue: It is lovely to see how many people enjoy watching the programme, and when a series finishes it's great to read the comments from people who say, 'We want more. Please hurry up and film some more, so we can see them.' And our family and friends have always loved watching us, and they've always been very supportive.

Also, they've told us after watching the programmes, 'You are who you are. That's how you come across. You don't try to make out that you're something that you're not.' That's nice to hear. But when you're being filmed constantly, like we are, you've just got to be yourself. There are actually times when you do forget that the camera is rolling and you're being filmed for a TV show. It just becomes part of your day – and that's another reason we come across as we do, because we are just being ourselves. The best thing to do is just go with it – and be yourself.

Noel: The reaction from people you don't know can be interesting. It's funny when we're out and about – just shopping or whatever – and before someone has walked past you, you can tell they've registered that it's us and are thinking, 'Hey, it's that family from the telly.' You daren't turn around because you know they're going to be looking. Sometimes people do come up to us and say, 'Hello, we've seen you on your programme' but with some people, they don't need to say anything – we just know from the way they look at us that they know who we are.

Sue: We absolutely love meeting people when we're out. If they come up to us and start chatting away it's really nice. It's nice that they have chosen to watch us on the TV, and it's nice that they've enjoyed it and want to pass that onto us. We're so pleased with the reaction to the show and the fact that it's so popular. I think the average viewing figures are something like 1.4 million.

Noel: But not everyone in the family has been keen to be on the show. Chris and Jack – you don't really see them, ever. The rest, though, have been fine about being on it.

Sue: With Chris and Jack, they're just quite shy when it comes to things like that – so they've never wanted to be on it, and you've got to respect them for that. It's not for everyone. It's a big thing, being seen by so many viewers. We always said from day one, 'If you don't want to be in it, that's absolutely fine. You're never going to be forced into doing something you don't want to do.'

Noel: On the other side of the coin, there have been some of the kids who really couldn't wait to be filmed – and it's changed over the years. One year it was Oscar and Casper who were up for doing anything and everything, then it was Hallie and Phoebe, then Max and Tillie – it changes all the time.

Everyone has their favourite episodes – I loved the one where you see Sue buying the motorhome without telling me! And I thought the episode when Luke came out as bisexual was a very good and a very moving one. And just some of the ones showing us on holiday – and me and Sue in the Maldives on our 30th wedding anniversary, that was good.

Sue: Like Noel, I think the buying the motorhome episode is right up there, and the Luke one I love – and the fact that he helped so many people doing that. It was a really lovely episode. I also loved the Christmas episode where we went to Lapland. With the motorhome one, it was just so funny because I'd been asking for one for so many years and I kept sending Noel links showing different ones – and he was like, 'Yeah, I'll have a think about it. I quite like this one and that one's OK.' Then I was like, 'Well, I've just bought one!'

Noel: Having made so many programmes now, we know far more than we used to about how TV shows are put together – because we knew nothing before! So that changes how we watch other programmes now – I wouldn't say it's ruined our viewing pleasure, but we sit there and will say, 'I know how they did that.'

If someone is being filmed going out of a front door – well, we know that person has had to do that twice. When you first watch something you think, 'God, there must be cameras everywhere' – but there's often probably only one, or maybe two at most. We've also learned that doing television involves a lot of standing around, doing nothing and just waiting. Then there's the length of time it can take to make a programme – a one-hour show could take a couple of months.

Sue: I don't think people realise how much work goes into making just one episode, which can involve a hell of a lot of filming. I think what's changed over the years is the media side of things. More recently, in particular, because the show has been getting more popular, the media don't seem to like that – so they have turned a bit, I'd say. But you're always going to get the negative side, so you just have to deal with it.

Noel: On the positive side, though, it's done great for the family pie business. It's almost like a free advert for it.

Sue: And best of all, as we've said, it's provided us with this fantastic family film scrapbook of memories – and you just can't beat that.

Noel: So, yes, 2012 was quite the year for me, Sue and the family – we welcomed Casper, our 16th child; Daisy, our first grandchild, and appeared on the telly for the first time. Everything was going well, including with the bakery – our business woes were well behind us now, and the future looked great all round.

Sue: I suppose you just never know when the worst, most heartbreaking news is around the corner. The next year – 2013 – was a relatively uneventful one for us, with no new additions to the family. Me and Noel did want more children, but we had no way of knowing that anything would be different for us in the future.

It's probably fair to say we didn't appreciate just how incredibly fortunate we were to have had 16 happy and healthy children. Don't get me wrong – no one thinks life is always going to be wonderful, but nothing could have prepared us for what we were about to go through, as a couple and as a family, in 2014.

Noel: It's so difficult for us to write about – so difficult for us to even think about. And yet, by writing about what happened to our family in that most difficult of years we can also pay a lasting tribute to the child we were never able to watch grow and develop. The child who will always be a part of our family – our family of 22 kids, not 21.

Sue: The next chapter is just for you, Alfie. We love you and we always will.

Chapter 9

In memory of Alfie

Alfie Thomas
Stillborn July 6, 2014
Due date November 11

Sue: From finding out I was pregnant with Alfie, I think I always knew we were never going to take him home. I just knew. It was so odd, because I'd never felt like that during any of my other pregnancies. But with Alfie, I somehow knew I wasn't going to take him home. Then, probably about three days prior to losing him, I just felt like he was slipping away because his movements were slowing down.

It began with my instincts and then, towards the end, it was little physical things I could feel – and I just knew that something really wasn't right. I had scans all the way through and, according to them, everything was totally fine. All the people we saw in the hospital thought everything was going to be OK. I remember a scan about two weeks before we lost him and we were told everything was fine – but I had such a weird feeling, such a bad feeling. Nobody on the medical side believed there was a problem until the day itself – all the scans had told them everything looked fine, which just shows how powerful an expectant mum's instincts can be.

I remember a few weeks before we lost him – I had this hand-held home heartbeat device for monitoring a baby's heartbeat, which I would actually never advise any mum-to-be to get. Anyway, on this particular occasion I couldn't find the heartbeat at all, so I panicked and phoned Noel at work. We then went to see the midwife at the Royal Lancaster Infirmary, who did find his heartbeat. Then, a few days before we lost Alfie, I was using the monitor again and his heartbeat was absolutely fine – but his movements had really slowed down. Then the day we lost him, we were filming down on the beach and I came home and I was getting some really sharp back pains and I said to Noel, 'I don't feel very well, and the baby's not really moved' – I'd only really felt him in the morning when I'd got up.

It got to teatime and I still hadn't felt anything so I thought we'd better go to the hospital. They couldn't find his heartbeat, either. Then the nurse came in with the scanning machine and she was scanning me – then she went to get a doctor. The doctor scanned me and that's when they said, 'We're really sorry but he's died.' Although I felt what I felt from the very start, I don't think you can ever be mentally prepared for something as awful as that happening to you. The fact that I had all those fears for so long didn't lessen the pain one bit. Finding out at the hospital that he had gone was just absolutely awful. It was terrible.

When I told the bereavement specialist midwife – a lovely woman called Celia Sykes – I didn't think I could get through it, she said, 'You WILL get through it. You've got your children and you WILL get through it.' But at that moment, I thought, 'I can't, I just can't.' I then got induced that night and Alfie was stillborn at half seven the following morning. It's hard because, obviously, you've got to try to carry on, day-to-day, for the kids, and we had a lot of kids, but I remember I didn't even go out of the house for about four weeks. It was just an awful time.

Unfortunately, it's very often the case that no one knows the reason why it happens. When Alfie was born, he looked absolutely perfect. I remember asking the midwife, 'Was there a knot in his umbilical cord or anything like that?' and she said, 'No, there was absolutely nothing.' He was perfect for his gestation – he was just short of 22 weeks – and his placenta was really healthy.

She said they could do a post-mortem or just some tests on the placenta. We didn't want a post-mortem – we wanted him just leaving as he was. So they never did that and it was probably about six weeks after we lost him that we had a consultant's appointment where he went through all the different things that could have happened. And he just said, 'I'm really sorry but we couldn't find any reason why his heartbeat stopped. Unfortunately, with stillborn births, you very often don't have a reason for why it happened.' I remember him also saying that, in some ways, that can be a good thing because if you do go on to have another child, the chances are they will be absolutely fine.

I never had those same instincts that I had with Alfie during any of the following pregnancies – and I didn't have them with any of the pregnancies before Alfie, so I think that really does show how powerful a mum-to-be's instincts can be. You don't realise how common it is for babies to be stillborn, as I discovered. When we shared the news that we had lost him, we got so many messages from people saying, 'I have been through the same thing' – it's unbelievable just how common it actually is.

But when you do have so many pregnancies that have been absolutely fine, you do take it for granted that the next one is going to be OK. But I think after we lost Alfie we definitely did then appreciate just how lucky we had been.

From the moment we lost him, we wanted Alfie's name to always be talked about. Obviously, the children born before Alfie were affected in different ways initially because they were different ages – some were so young they didn't understand what had happened. And of course, the ones who came after Alfie had to find out from us what had happened to their brother.

Just a few days after each of them were born, we took them to Alfie's grave with the older children. We visit his grave frequently as a family and that has always been really important for me and Noel. The children have never forgotten about Alfie – he has always been a part of the family, and the children who have come along after Alfie all know about him.

For me, the build-up to Alfie's birthday is always really, really hard. The actual day itself is not quite as bad – it somehow seems more peaceful. My mood is a lot lower about a week or so before the day. I was in a foul mood before Alfie's last birthday – and I knew exactly why I was. I suppose people just deal with it differently, because I know it's the actual day that is the worst time for Noel.

We always go to Alfie's grave on his birthday, take flowers and just sit with him for a while. Sometimes, we've let balloons off as well. We will sit and talk to him. For Alfie's last birthday, the kids took a fruit yoghurt and a chocolate bar up for him, bless them.

At first, we couldn't find a graveyard where we wanted him to be and it was the funeral directors, Robert and Kathryn Caunce, who said, 'What about this one?' It was Hale Carr Cemetery in Heysham. Alfie is right on top of a hill, and he can look right over and see Williamson Park in Lancaster. It's such a beautiful spot. As soon as we saw it, we knew that was the place we wanted him to be.

It's really strange but when you're planning your child's funeral, you just don't think about things like that at first. But we were really fussy about where we wanted him to be, and we were so grateful that the funeral directors suggested the place that we decided on. It's perfect.

Me, Noel and all the family think about Alfie all the time. When I think about him, I imagine him running around in heaven with my dad, and I imagine him having blond hair, like Casper, because his hair was blond when he was born. And I've had readings done by people since he passed, and since my dad passed, and one of the things I heard was, 'There's a gentleman and a boy, with blond hair, and the man – your dad – wants you to know he's looking after him for you.' It was comforting to hear that. I also think about what his interests would have been – I always think, being in between Casper and Hallie, he would have been playing with Oscar and Casper.

It's quite hard, because our Sophie's daughter, Ayprill, is the same age as Alfie – she was born on October 13, 2014, and Alfie had been due to be born on November 11, 2014. So, when Ayprill is having her birthday, you're thinking again about how Alfie would have been enjoying his birthday soon afterwards.

The kids are always surprising us – and delighting us – by coming out with things and doing things relating to Alfie. Oscar, when he was about five, took his favourite toy cars – that he never ever parted with – to put on Alfie's grave. And he said, 'I'm leaving these here for Alfie.' That was so lovely. Those cars stayed there for ages, because Oscar wanted his little brother to enjoy them.

If another set of parents, who had just been through the same thing as we had with Alfie, asked us for advice, I'd definitely say, 'Make sure you take lots of pictures of the baby and have them as your memories. And be assured that as low as you are now – and it's the lowest you will ever be – things WILL get better. You'll never, ever forget but you will just learn to cope with it.'

I remember, probably about three years after we lost Alfie, I had a lovely lady message me, and she said, 'I've just found out my little girl has passed away and I've got to go into hospital to give birth to her' – and I said to her, 'Please, please take as many pictures as you can possibly take. You're going to be really upset, and might not feel like you want to take those pictures of you and your daughter, but please take those pictures of her because you will cherish them forever.'

She messaged me shortly after her daughter was stillborn and said, 'I just want to say thank you so much for your advice – we took lots of pictures with her and I just wanted to thank you for taking the time out.' I also have Alfie's handprints and footprints on a necklace. And I have a tattoo of Alfie's footprints on my left foot, so he's always walking with me.

He's always going to be part of the family – we always say, 'We have 22 kids.' That's how we feel. Alfie is a huge part of the family and that will always be the case.

Noel: Sue never said to me, as she was going through the pregnancy, that she felt she wouldn't be taking a baby home from the hospital. She kept all those feelings and fears to herself. But once Alfie had died, Sue told me, 'I knew I was never going to bring him home.' If she had shared that, it might have been a little bit easier for her during the pregnancy – but I know she simply didn't want to worry or upset me.

Sue does hide stuff well. There probably were a few times when she said, 'Something doesn't feel quite right' but I think because we had been very lucky in the past, I just assumed everything was going to be fine. It didn't really cross my mind that something was going to go so terribly wrong.

It was just awful. Absolutely awful. Sue and I suffered terribly – but the whole family has, too. All the kids – even though it would have been at different times, because of their ages – have suffered. It's taken a long, long time to come to terms with what happened – and we still get upset. The younger kids, at the time, obviously didn't understand what had happened – Oscar and Casper were very young then and didn't have a clue what was going on. But then you've got the older ones who did – especially Luke and Millie, who I think it affected the most. They were really upset.

We knew about Hale Carr Cemetery but, for some reason, had never really thought about it for Alfie. It's a really lovely place. The views are just magnificent. The other places we saw – one was near a motorway, so that was out, while another, well, it just wasn't nice. Hale Carr is in a great position, and I'll drive past on my way to work and say 'Good morning' to Alfie.

With Alfie's birthday, unlike Sue, I think it's more the day itself that I find really difficult, rather than the build-up. But the visits to his grave are so special – on his birthday and throughout the year. It's so important that we are always thinking about him and always talking about him. He is one of our 22 children and always will be.

Thinking about Alfie since he died, I'm just the same as Sue.

I picture this boy with blond hair, looking a bit like Casper and Oscar. I'm not into all the readings that Sue mentioned, but it is interesting and it's nice to hear that.

In the hospital, we never thought about taking photographs of Alfie. The people in the hospital took some for us, then we took some ourselves. It didn't even cross our minds to take them. But I'm really glad they mentioned it. And as well as the photographs, I'd also advise people in the same situation to do the little handprints and footprints of your baby as well.

With Alfie, because of his gestation – just short of 22 weeks – we didn't get a birth certificate or a death certificate. The hospital gave us their own version of one – but stillborn babies have to be 24 weeks before you can actually register them. What happened with Alfie was absolutely awful and it broke our hearts. But he will forever be a big part of our family – because he is one of our 22 kids, and always will be.

Chapter 10

Hallie

Hallie Alphia Beau
Born June 3, 2015

Sue: Right after we lost Alfie, regarding the thought of having more children, I was just thinking, 'No, I can't. I just can't put myself through that again.' But then, a little bit later, I thought, 'Do you know, I'd really love to have another one.' There was obviously that fear of going through what we went through before. But after I'd had that meeting with the consultant, I felt a lot more reassured – not least about the care I would receive after what happened with Alfie.

But the pregnancies after Alfie were all very different to the ones before. I was a lot more on edge. I took Aspirin throughout the pregnancies because the consultant said that could help.

I was induced with Hallie, going into hospital just coming

up to 38 weeks. She'd had a really quiet day and I remember lying on the sofa, thinking, 'I just want this baby out. I can't deal with the stress of it and I feel absolutely awful.' I went in and they checked her over and found she was absolutely fine. But they agreed with me – they said, 'We're going to induce her, and just get this baby out safely.' And that's what they did.

I was lucky because I had a really supportive consultant who really listened to my concerns – and then when I got to 38 or 39 weeks during the pregnancies after Alfie, they would never let me go over that and induced me, which was good because I think if I had got to 40 weeks I would have just been an absolute nervous wreck.

With Hallie, I was always scanned frequently – and that was so good in keeping me grounded. I was a lot less anxious and a lot less nervous because of that. I was still anxious, but nowhere near as bad as I would have been without the frequent scans or the great care I received at the Royal Lancaster Infirmary. It made such a big difference to me. The care was absolutely fantastic.

I remember just after Hallie was born, she was placed on me and I said to Noel, 'We did it!' The relief was just amazing. We were so, so happy and so, so grateful. You never know how a pregnancy is going to go – you are never guaranteed to bring that baby home – and we had obviously been through such a dreadful, awful time with Alfie. But when Hallie arrived, it was a simply wonderful moment.

Noel: After Alfie died, like Sue, I felt reassured when we were told by the consultant that just because it had happened once that didn't mean it was going to happen again. I think me and Sue were both on the same page regarding our feelings about having another child after Alfie. We decided we definitely wanted another one. But at the same time we were very nervous – well, scared, really – about what could go wrong. Having lost Alfie, we were always pushing for going into hospital after 38 weeks during the following pregnancies.

The care that Sue got after Alfie was just brilliant. And by now we'd got friendly with a lady who had her own private scanner and she always said to Sue, 'Come in whenever you want and we will reassure you.' We did that, and it was really good. I think when Hallie was born, it was a 'Thank God you are here!' moment. The feelings of relief and utter joy were just fantastic.

Sue: Hallie weighed 7lb 3oz, but because she was two weeks early she was quite a good weight. Her middle name is Alphia, and that is in tribute to Alfie. We wanted her to have a version of Alfie's name as her middle name, which is why we chose that name.

Noel: All the kids were excited to welcome Hallie home – as they were with all the babies – and like us, I think they were just relieved to see her.

Sue: Hallie was an easy baby and slept through from about three months old, which is really, really good. She's quite mischievous – quite a character!

Noel: She's a bit like Sophie and Millie. I could see her, perhaps, getting in trouble at school for talking. She was a bit slow in getting going at school, but she then excelled herself all of a sudden and her teachers were saying to us that her Maths ability had really blossomed.

Sue: She also loves a bit of dance, she's got loads of friends she always plays out with – and she loves crafts, so is always colouring and drawing.

Noel: She also loves going out on her bike. She can be quite shy at times, but I think once she gets to know people the shyness goes.

Chapter 11

Pie Heaven
(Part Two)

Noel: Having endured such terrible times relatively early in our business life, when our plans to open a second shop ended in debt and despair, it was lovely to be able to celebrate a significant development in November 2015 – the online launch of The Radfords Pie Company.

We were thrilled and – helped by our higher profile, now that we were "that big family on the TV" – the business went from strength to strength. In fact, we recently had the bunting out again for another magnificent milestone – the 25th anniversary of the business! We're so proud of that, and so pleased that we're still here – still trading and doing so well, after coming through an extremely testing period.

We've worked very hard – all of us. It's a real family affair, because of all the effort that me, Sue and all the older kids have put in over the years. We had to make a lot of sacrifices at the beginning when we were fighting to establish the business – and simply keep it going – after setting up shop in Heysham on February 12 1999. We have already revisited the nightmare era when we foolishly opened a second shop in Kendal. There weren't any holidays in the early years of the business, and things were often incredibly tight regarding money – as well as being very stressful.

For a good while we seemed to be skint all the time, but to have turned it around like we did and for all that hard work to have paid off is so pleasing.

Sue: We're also proud of the success we made of the business after those very difficult years because, having been in the public eye now for a good while, you do get people who really don't like you and do their damnedest to try to ruin your business. It's sad to know there are people like that out there, but we know there are – because they have been behind fake reviews and negative comments which can only be designed to damage our company. It's been really difficult for us to deal with.

Noel: It's a double-edged sword, being on the telly. There's the positive side of increased sales, which we know have undoubtedly come from our higher profile because some of the people who place online orders tell us they did so after seeing us on the box, and there is always a spike in sales during the screening of a series. The pros definitely outweigh the cons, but Sue is right – there is a negative side because of those spiteful people who, for some warped reason, want to harm our business and our family.

Sue: I don't know whether it's jealousy or just spitefulness, but some people really have it in for us and their unkindness has attempted to damage our business. They basically want to see you fail in life. We've known them to write fake reviews, leave hurtful and untrue comments.

But I'm really, really proud of all the obstacles we've overcome and how well the business is now doing. When we set up online in 2015, I remember we had a meeting with the website designer. He said, 'I'm not sure about this. I don't know if it's going to do well or not.' But I was convinced it would succeed because everything was starting to move online back then. So, we went ahead and launched it – and it got really big really quickly.

We later got to the point where we had to open a new, bigger bakehouse – replacing the one attached to the shop – in September 2021. I'm also proud that, because it is a family business, it will always be there for the kids should they want to work for it, as a lot of them already have.

Noel: The new bakehouse isn't huge – it's probably about 1,000 square feet – but it must be nearly three times the size of the one that was next to the shop.

Sue: I used to make the pies with Noel. I used to block out the pies, fill them, put the lids on and so on. And I'll be going back to that soon when our youngest, Heidie, starts school. I've not worked there for a long time – I think it was when I was pregnant with Oscar in 2011 that I stopped working.

I love pies, but Noel never brings them home! My favourite is the chicken and gammon one – I absolutely love it. I think Noel doesn't bring them home because he's surrounded by pies all the time and makes them all day, so he's just sick of the sight of them. But come on Noel, bring some pies home!

Noel: Isn't there a saying about never bringing your work home with you? I'm very proud of the pies we make but yes, I think people get sick of whatever they're faced with all the time at work – people who work in a chocolate factory will be sick of chocolate and so on. We make so many different pies. The Incredibly Meaty range includes meat and potato, steak, steak and stilton, steak and ale, steak and mushroom, peppered steak, steak and kidney, minced beef and onion, chicken, chicken and gammon and chicken and mushroom. There's also cheese and onion for vegetarians and we do a green Thai vegetable one for vegans – it's really nice but just not popular enough to keep it on sale all the time. We also do a range at Christmas, which includes turkey, cranberry and stuffing, and beef with red wine. Then there are three ploughman-style pork pies – one with cheese in the middle and a pickle on top, another with cranberry sauce on top, and one with apple and cider chutney on top. Our biggest sellers are steak and mushroom, peppered steak and chicken and gammon. I've not got any analytics set up to see which parts of the country order the most pies, but I bet it's the North of England – though I'm sure there are a lot of exiled north-erners in the South who order them because they miss a good pie. And I'm proud to say we get a lot of people from Wigan – described by many as the country's Pie Capital – travelling to our shop to buy our pies, so we must be doing something right! I think we sell maybe around 260,000 pies a year. In the shop, there are three people – including our Aimee – and there are five in the bakery, including me, Chloe, Jack and Luke. We'll produce hundreds of pies a day, but the exact amount can vary a great deal – it all depends what we're working on, because some of the pies are more time-consuming to make than others.

It's good being self-employed, because we can choose, to a certain extent, when we work. But our work in the bakehouse will tend to start around 6.30am, and be over by 2.30pm. Then again, the work does come home with me sometimes. There's still stuff I need to deal with at home – emails and so on.

Sue: And when Noel goes away on holiday, it's not a proper break for him because he will still be having to deal with emails and ordering things. But we're so glad to have the business – for us and the kids.

Noel: It's nine of the kids who have worked for the business over the years. Daniel was there for the shortest time – when he was in between jobs. But with the others, it's been for quite a while – and they've all been really good workers, because I think they understand it's their name above the door. They do take pride in that, and they're certainly not skivers.

Anyway, I think it's time we heard from Chloe, Jack and Luke – who work in the bakehouse – and Aimee, who works in the shop. Taking into account her time at university and being on maternity leave, Chloe has worked for the business for about 10 years, off and on – but mostly on. Jack and Luke both started about three years ago, while Aimee has been in the shop for more than a year now.

So, let's see what they've got to say for themselves…

* * *

Chloe: I really enjoy working in the bakery – and I've always enjoyed working with dad. Now I've got two of my brothers here as well, so it's even better. If dad isn't here, because I know the process so well, Jack and Luke will listen to anything I need to say during the day and they'll just get on with it. There's no rivalry. It's professional here but it's also very relaxed, because we all know what we're doing and get on so well. And dad is as chilled-out at work as he is at home – I've never known anyone like him! He never lets anything bother him, so I think that makes the work environment better as well.

Jack: I've been here since January 2021. It's good working here, we all just get our heads down and get on with it. We'll get all the orders in, tally them all up and do what has to be done that day. We all work really well together, and some days we can be finished by 1pm. It's busy but it's not stressful. It's more relaxing working with family – in an ordinary company, you obviously don't get to pick and choose who you're working with and if you don't like working with a particular person it can make it not a very nice place to work. Here, we're family and we all get on.

Luke: Working here, in a family business, is so different to the working environment in a 'normal' job. It's much more laid-back, you can communicate more easily with people and it just flows a lot better. Obviously, though, working with your dad comes with its own disadvantages – you can't pull a sickie for example! But working with family, everyone knows each other and there's none of that having to learn all about someone new. I wouldn't say there is any sibling rivalry. Chloe was here before me and Jack, and though we do answer to dad – if he isn't here, then Chloe is next in line because of how long she's worked here so it would just be natural to listen to her.

Aimee: I love working for my dad – he's definitely a good boss. I've been in the shop for more than a year. I love meeting and serving people – and you get quite a few customers, who have seen the TV programme, asking if they can have a picture. That's really nice. It's great to have our name above the door and it's really special working for the family business – I love it. It's great for all the children to know that the business is here if they need it. I'd like to work in the bakery as well at some point, but eventually I'd like to do hairdressing full-time.

* * *

Noel: What a team – no wonder the business is doing so well! We do enter the British Pie Awards and have won silvers and bronzes – it would be nice to get a gold one day. Most importantly, it's lovely to know we have so many happy customers. We get a lot of nice comments from people after they've tried the pies for the first time. And it's nice being in the bakehouse and seeing the orders flowing in. The online business is doing so well. We had an order from someone recently for 300 pies! But though we'll get quite a few asking for 30 or 40, the average order is for about eight to 15 pies. The minimum order is six, because it's just not worth it otherwise with the shipping costs.

As I say, we get a lot of orders because people have seen the TV programme – and the shop benefits in the same way. Aimee tells us about people visiting the shop who have come from as far away as the North East and Scotland. If other people from far and wide who are reading this want to pop into the shop while they're in the area, I'd better let them know when it's open! They can buy their pies at 376 Heysham Road, Heysham between 8am and 2pm Monday to Friday, and 8am and 1pm on Saturday.

Things are going very well with the shop, the bakehouse and the online business, but I don't think me and Sue will ever go down the road of opening a second shop again because of the experience we had in Kendal. The memories are still raw all these years on, and it would be just too much of a risk. I think a better way forward would be getting as many of our pies as possible into as many outlets as possible, via wholesalers. And if we do end up doing that, then it could mean getting a bigger industrial unit or, alternatively, having a 24-hour production operation.

Sue: That is definitely something we're looking at. But don't forget, Noel, there's another thing you need to sort out.

Noel: What's that?

Sue: Start bringing some pies home!

Chapter 12

Phoebe and Archie

Phoebe Willow
Born July 24, 2016

Sue: I think we should take the opportunity to pause and reflect here, before talking about Phoebe and Archie. I can understand some readers may already have felt overwhelmed by the size of our family and how, in this book, the children just keep on coming – as they did for me and Noel! From our point of view, it's definitely not a numbers game. We appreciate people may be thinking, 'Wow! Phoebe is your 19th! Archie is your 20th! That's just unbelievable!' But although we're honestly more aware than anyone about the size of our family, we don't dwell on the numbers involved. We just loved having children. We loved the fact we were given a second chance after Noel's vasectomy reversal – and we were grateful that we were able to find the strength to conquer our fears about having further children after we tragically lost Alfie. Anyway, let's now talk about lovely Phoebe and lovely Archie! Phoebe was a straightforward labour – no problems at all – and weighed 7lb 6oz. She is our wild child – a bit of a daredevil! She's just got no fear at all. When we go to theme parks and water parks, she wants to go on everything – whatever it may be. She is such a character, and I think she will continue with that daredevil attitude as she gets older.

Noel: It's probably a good outlook to have on life – just try things, and if you don't like them then try something else. And she absolutely loves animals – anything and everything in the animal world.

Sue: Phoebe wants to be a vet when she gets older and I could see her doing that. She just loves animals, and she's not scared of any of them. She once had an animal-themed birthday party and we had a load of different things in the house – including a snake, which she wasn't bothered about at all. She even had a tarantula on her head – she just isn't frightened of anything.

Archie Rowan
Born: September 18, 2017

Sue: Calling him 'Archie' wasn't because the name begins and ends with the same letters as 'Alfie' does, and because he was the first boy after Alfie. We just loved the name, but it was a nice coincidence. And it was definitely special, having the first boy after Alfie. I think I was a little bit more worried about his pregnancy because I knew we were having a boy. I think with Hallie's pregnancy – if she had been a boy, I would have probably worried a lot more, after what happened with Alfie.

The fact that she was a girl made it easier, maybe – and it was the same with Phoebe. But Archie was fine – he was 8lb 14oz, second only in weight to Katie, who was 9lb 3oz. The labour was fine, and there were no problems at all. He was a good baby, too. But I would say Archie is definitely one of our more challenging children – let's put it that way! If something doesn't go his way, then he is quite difficult to talk down. If he isn't allowed to do something, then he isn't happy.

Noel: He's not one for sharing.

Sue: But he's been really good at school and he loves school. He's got lots of friends and is doing well with his reading and his writing.

Noel: He's a very lovable lad – and loves his brothers and sisters. But it's just that if he doesn't get what he wants, or something is frustrating him, he'll start crying and things like that. But he's still only young and he will grow out of it.

Sue: He loves going out on bike rides, loves football and loves doing crafts and drawing and things.

Noel: Just eight days after Archie was born, me and Sue celebrated our silver wedding anniversary – so that September was a very special month for us. After a very difficult start to our relationship – before we even got up the aisle! – we were now able to celebrate 25 years of happy marriage, and the birth of our 20th child. And by then, we also had four grandchildren – Daisy, Ayprill, Leo and Maisie. Just wonderful!

Sue: We were so, so thankful!

Chapter 13

Now we're on YouTube!

Sue: We decided to launch our own YouTube channel at the start of 2018 – and I think it was my idea. I said, 'What about doing YouTube?' because I thought it would be quite good to do our everyday life in the form of these vlogs – also known as video blogs and video logs. Obviously a lot of people enjoy watching the programme – but when the programme isn't on, I thought it would be good to fill the gap with our own videos. And I'll tell you, when you're doing it all yourself it's very different to being filmed by a camera crew.

   Noel: Especially because I'm rubbish at it – and if we're in a public space, I will NOT hold the camera and point it at myself and talk.

   Sue: He absolutely hates it! And yet when you're out with a camera crew, Noel, you're perfectly fine – you just don't like doing it when you're on your own, or there is no crew with you.

I don't mind it myself, I think I've got used to it over the years. It's also good with the YouTube videos, because they're more immediate – you can do something and get it uploaded really quickly, whereas obviously the TV process takes a lot longer.

Noel: Some YouTubers out there will have a set plan and timetable – they'll say, 'We're going to do this, this and this.' Ours is just a case of, 'Should we vlog today? What shall we do then?'

Sue: What I'm really conscious of, though, is if we have a really busy filming schedule for the TV show, then I don't feel like I want to pick the camera up and vlog with the kids because I feel on the days we're not filming they should be days off for us all – so we're not constantly having a camera in our faces. For me, I'm quite strict on that. If we're away for a weekend, in the motorhome or whatever, then we'll vlog that – but if we're having a few days off in the week where we're not filming then we just won't film. Me and Noel might film a simple Q&A or something like that, but we wouldn't film the kids. We do enjoy doing it, it's good fun and it's nice to look back on these memories as well, because the vlogging is a bit different to what we do with the television programmes.

Noel: The kids quite enjoy it, too – there are a few of them that will pick the camera up and have a go. It's some of the older ones and some of the younger ones – a bit of a mixture. It just depends what mood they're in to be honest. But out of us two, I think it's Sue who's the most natural with the camera – but I do hold the camera more steady!

Sue: I always get moaned at for not keeping the camera still!

Noel: What is interesting is when we've made a video and you start to think about how many people might watch it – sometimes you'll be really sure about one of them and you'll be really surprised that it doesn't get the figures you imagined it would. It's sometimes hard to tell which ones will be the most popular. You can do one which you think is a normal, everyday video and it will surprise you by doing really, really well.

Sue: We always knew that the house tour ones would get a lot of viewers because people are naturally nosey aren't they? And the ones showing Noel cooking always do well – but Noel hates doing them and I have to persuade him! I think they do particularly well because people like to save money, and Noel does ones which show how you can feed a family cheaply. The thing is, Noel is really good at doing them – and I think he'd be good at doing his own cookery show.

Noel: It just seems weird talking to a camera on my own – I've never got used to that.

Sue: The viewing figures are just amazing – the first house tour we did has so far got something like 1.3 million views. And in total, over the whole channel – we've made more than 450 videos – we have had around 71 million views! We're really proud of the channel, and delighted to have 365,000 subscribers.

Noel: There is a big range of material on it but we're not very organised. We should get a big plan together. It is a business at the end of the day, but we don't really treat it like one – we treat it as a bit of fun. If it brings a bit of income in at the same time, then great – it's a bit of a win-win. There are sponsored videos, where companies pay a certain amount for you to showcase a product – for example, I did a cookery video where I used a particular pressure cooker, so we were paid for featuring that and given the pressure cooker and pans to go with it as well. Then the normal family videos – of a birthday party, a trip in the motorhome or whatever – will have advert breaks in them, and that generates revenue for us. You can either have adverts put in or not put in, and you can have things set so YouTube will do it automatically – and it will put the ads in where it thinks they work best.

Sue: We don't know what the figures are for the adverts.

Noel: It's called the YouTube CPM, which is the price advertisers pay content creators like us for every 1,000 views an ad receives on YouTube. And you can put up as many or as few videos as you like – you can put up just one a month if you want.

Sue: I love the birthday videos and it's nice to be able to look back at the videos from when the little ones were born. And I like Noel's cookery ones as well.

Noel: I like the house tours – it's nice to look back at the house in Morecambe and see how much work we've done on it. I also like the holiday ones when we're all having a good time – they're nice to look back on. And the birthday ones, too. Also, with your own platforms – like YouTube – it's good because you will get a positive response. And if there is an idiot on there writing something stupid, you can just remove it – or block them. We're in total control because it's our channel, and we can edit things however we like.

Sue: Yeah, it's just lovely to have that control with our own social media platforms. We really enjoy having a YouTube channel – we've never regretted it. It was my idea, wasn't it, Noel?

Noel: Yes, Sue, it was your idea – but I still say you're too shaky with the camera!

Chapter 14

Bonnie and Heidie and... No, that's it for us!

Bonnie Raye
Born November 6, 2018

Sue: Ah, Noel, it feels quite sad to have got to the point in the book where we're introducing our last two children.

Noel: I know what you mean, Sue, but we couldn't go on forever!

Sue: Bonnie was 7lb 14oz – a good labour, and she slept through from quite an early age.

Noel: She's such a happy child. She's always laughing. She has such a cheerful nature and always seems to be happy and smiley.

Sue: She loves crafts and drawing and colouring – and her dolls, too. She also loves going out on her bike, and she loves our trips in the motorhome. And she doesn't get stressed out in the same way Archie does. In fact, Bonnie is so laid-back, I'd say she is horizontal! She doesn't seem to let anything bother her. It's incredible how some kids can be so close together in age and yet be so different in their characters and personalities. They can be so similar in so many ways, but just so different in others.

Heidie Rose
Born April 3, 2020

Sue: Here we are – talking about our 22nd child; our last child, which means Heidie will forever be the youngest in the family, and the baby of the family. She was actually born at the beginning of the first Covid lockdown.

Noel: We weren't even sure if I was going to be allowed in when Sue was ready to go into labour. But luckily, the Royal Lancaster said the partner was allowed in. I don't think that was the case everywhere during Covid.

Sue: I did have my scans and other hospital appointments on my own because Noel wasn't allowed, and it was really stressful because of the whole lockdown situation. But it all worked out fine in the end. Heidie weighed 6lb 15oz. It was hard when we got home because, when you have a new baby you want to be able to show him or her to all your friends and family straight away and we couldn't do that this time. I remember saying to the midwife, 'I'm OK because we've got a really big family at home but I really, really feel for those new mums who aren't going to be able to have family around and will feel totally isolated.' I also remember saying I thought there'd be a lot of new mums ending up with postnatal depression because of that, and she said, 'It's funny you should say that because we were just having that conversation this morning, and we think the same thing.'

Noel: Heidie is definitely a mummy's girl – she was breastfed until she was two-and-a-half. It was more Heidie than Sue who didn't want to give up!

Sue: She loves playing with Bonnie – those two are really close. She loves nursery, drawing and playing with her dolls and tea set. And she'll always be special – and mummy's baby – because she's the last one.

You may have noticed she has the same middle name – Rose – as our first daughter, Sophie.

Noel: We picked Rose for Sophie because my mum's middle name was Rose – and we thought it would be nice, as Heidie is our last child, to finish with a Rose.

* * *

22 Kids... the counting has stopped (not including grandchildren!)

Noel: I think me and Sue are both the same. When we decided Heidie would be the last one, we were ready for that – but then, as she was getting older, you started to think, 'We won't need the cot anymore, and we won't need the pram anymore, and there are no more bottles.' You sort of noticed these things and thought, 'Ah, we won't have that ever again.'

Sue: But then we thought, 'We won't have nappies anymore!' It's amazing, though, to look back and think, 'We've had 22 kids – 11 boys and 11 girls.' What are the chances of that? It could so easily have been, say, 15 boys, or 15 girls, rather than 11 of each.

Noel: I think we got to at least 17 or 18 kids and we didn't even realise what the ratio was ourselves. Perhaps we were just too busy! But if it was all lads, it would have been all right. If it was all girls, I think I would have left home a long time ago!

Sue: Oh my God – the hormones! Oh my word! Boys are definitely a lot easier than girls – girls are a lot more highly-strung, while boys just get on with things. After our experiences, I can definitely say that is the case – the boys have been easier.

Noel: All the cliches are right about kids when they go through puberty and become teenagers – they're horrible! Though some are more horrible than others. If you look at Max, he's a teenager – but there have been no problems with him at all.

Sue: Max has definitely been the easiest out of all of them. I think it's just because Max is very laid-back, just gets on with it and doesn't let anything bother him, which is amazing when you think he's got autism.

Noel: Thinking back to their very early days, Chloe was the most difficult for that period when she had colic at a few months old. But that didn't last. Some, meanwhile, have been a bit testing at school.

Sue: The one who has changed most is Josh – he was an absolute nightmare for a good few years. It was hard to get him to go to school, but then he was totally different as soon as he went to college. He's grown up a lot and is just much happier in himself.

With the girls, people often mention their names and how they all end with an 'e' – and honestly, that was something we never realised until we got to... I think it was Ellie or Aimee, and they were our fifth and sixth girls! Then someone asked, 'Is there a reason your girls' names all end with an 'e'? We just hadn't realised. But then when it was pointed out, we thought, 'Yes, let's keep it like that.' But luckily, we did like the names that had that sound anyway.

But thinking about having 11 of each – I'm extremely happy with that. I wouldn't have wanted it any other way – more girls or more boys. We just feel so incredibly lucky. We were heartbroken to lose Alfie, but he will always be a part of our family – and all his brothers and sisters are happy and healthy. You can't ask for any more than that.

Noel: I second all of that, Sue. We really are amazingly lucky parents.

Chapter 15

What every woman wants to know from a Mum–of–22... but is afraid to ask!

Sue: In my eyes, I'm just a normal mum – but I do understand that, in the eyes of a great many other women, I'm anything but. The thing is, everyone gets used to their own lives and their own circumstances – which is why I sometimes have to take a step back and say to myself, 'Wow! I've had 22 children!'

It is something that I understand fascinates a lot of people – not least other women and, perhaps, especially other mums and mums-to-be. Mums who haven't had 22 children! Over the years I have been asked so many varied questions about my life as a mum, though I know some women have been shy about asking me certain things. This chapter is for them, as well as all those mums who weren't backward in coming forward to ask me particular things – some quite personal! I've collected together a wide selection of some of the questions I have been asked – often by perfect strangers who, I'm pleased to say, are fans of our show on Channel 5.

But as you'll see, one or two of the more personal questions also call for an answer from Noel. Come on Noel, get over here – this involves you, too!

Fire away, ladies...

You must have had various cravings for different types of food during at least some of your pregnancies – can you remember what they were, and did they create any problems (not least for Noel, who might have had a problem getting hold of them)?

Sue: With Chris, our first, I never really had any cravings as such, though I did used to like having a lot of ice lollies – which I think was because I had terrible morning sickness. But then, for the rest of them, I had a really weird craving – for flour, of all things! Looking back now, I know it sounds awful – and it IS awful! I think it was the texture that appealed to me for some reason.

Noel: Flour – straight out of the bag! But you did have another craving, too – for pickled onions.

Sue: Oh yeah, I did – with Chris. I'd forgotten all about that. It was ice lollies in the beginning, until I got to about five or six months, and then after that it was pickled onions. Then, with the rest of them, I never really wanted to have pickled onions – just flour! And it wasn't just a bit of flour, I had to have quite a bit.

Noel: I remember you would be sitting in the living room with a little bag of flour – or maybe not so little! You certainly married the right person – a baker!

Sue: It was so random, but at least it was easy to get hold of!

Did you bottle-feed or breast-feed your babies? I really do hope, for your sake, you didn't breast-feed so many children! And what would your advice to new mums be on this subject? Any regrets about your own choice?

Sue: With Chris, I didn't want to breast-feed – so I bottle-fed him. Then, when I had Sophie, I thought, 'Oh, I'm going to try breast-feeding.' I breast-fed Sophie for about three weeks before going onto the bottle – but the rest of them have all been breast-fed, for different lengths of time. As I said earlier in the book, Max was a nightmare to breast-feed because he put his tongue up to the top of his mouth and his jaw was set back. I had to change to bottles with him after about a week. And I remember Hallie was initially difficult to breast-feed because her jawline was a little bit set back, as well, but I persevered and we got there in the end and I think I breast-fed her for probably about four months. The last time, with Heidie, she was about two-and-a-half when she stopped breast-feeding!

I know there may be a lot of women reading this, and thinking, 'Wow, that's a lot of breast-feeding, over so many years' – but, for me, I really liked it because I liked the closeness it gives you. But also, formula is just so expensive. I always say to our kids who are having their own babies that 'fed is best' – whether it's bottle-fed or breast-fed it doesn't matter, as long as they are fed. And don't feel guilty if you don't breast-feed, because it's not for everybody, is it? What I did worked for me and I've no regrets, but I would never, ever tell any other mums what they should or shouldn't do. With our kids, I've heard, 'Ah, I don't really want to breast-feed' and I've said, 'That's fine, if you don't want to give it a go, then don't give it a go.'

What pain relief did you have – pethidine, gas and air or epidurals? I loved gas and air. Would you prefer a canister of gas and air on a Friday night instead of a glass of wine?

Sue: I love gas and air! That stuff is just amazing, it really is. I bet loads of mums would say the same thing. With Chris, I had pethidine and gas and air but the pethidine really knocked me out. I thought it was awful, so that was the end of that for me. When I was having Sophie, I did say, 'No, I'm not having that pethidine' so I just had gas and air – and I found that was all I needed for the labour. I've never had any epidurals, so I realise I have been very fortunate there. As for whether I'd be tempted by a canister of gas and air on a Friday night instead of a glass of wine... definitely! It's simply amazing stuff. Did you ever try it, Noel?

  Noel: Once, when the midwife had left the room! I quite enjoyed it, too!

Did your waters ever break when you were out and about? Were there any embarrassing/funny situations before you got to the safety of the hospital?

Sue: My waters broke at home with Sophie and she was born about an hour afterwards, and my waters broke just as I was leaving the house with Katie – and she was a labour of about 10 minutes! But I do have another really funny story about my waters breaking – in addition to the one with Daniel when I was in the car outside Asda while Noel was inside buying his snacks and casually chatting to a neighbour! So, when I was having Millie I was just lying on the bed and I think the midwife thought that my waters had gone – but you can have your hind-waters going first, which is just a slow trickle (this can happen if the hole in the membranes is small or not directly in front of the baby's head). But I think the midwife thought that was it and they'd gone, and she was saying, 'You can start pushing now.' I started pushing – and my waters just exploded in her face. She was absolutely covered! I was laughing, even though I was trying to push this baby out. The bed was soaking wet – the midwife was soaking wet, and it was just an incredible, hilarious scene! The midwife, I remember, was just standing there – dripping wet, because she's got my waters all over her – and this other midwife ended up coming in the room, and said to her, 'Oh, do you need to go and get changed?' And off she went to get changed and get herself dry.

Noel: We didn't see her again!

Sue: It was so funny, and before she left she had said to me, 'I have never, ever had that happen to me before.' I also remember saying – through all the commotion, and the laughter and the water being everywhere – 'Put the brakes on the bed!' Because the bed was moving everywhere. It was the funniest thing I ever went through.

What was the shortest time you were in labour – and what was the longest?

Sue: Chris was the longest, at about 26 hours, and Katie was the shortest – I think the labour time for Katie was officially recorded at 11 minutes.

Did you give Noel plenty of abuse while giving birth? And was Noel always able to be by your side?

Sue: Yes, Noel was always by my side, I'm pleased to say. But no, I don't think I ever gave him any abuse while I was giving birth. But if he started talking absolute waffle, and I was having a contraction, I was like, 'For goodness' sake, Noel, shut up!'

Noel: But you've never given me stick, have you? Though you have told me off for sleeping in the delivery room!

Sue: Yeah, you always went to sleep! Always asleep in the chair while I was having my contractions! I was thinking, 'What are you doing? I'm trying to push a baby out and you've nodded off!'

Noel: No, I was always awake for the important bit, the nitty gritty bit – for the birth, itself. I wasn't nodding off all the way through.

Sue: And he always had to buy his snacks before we got to the hospital.

Noel: I'm actually convinced that the chair they provide for dads is the most uncomfortable chair there is – and they use that one on purpose, so you can't sleep.

Sue: But you didn't have a problem – you WERE able to sleep. You were always nodding off!

Noel: Yeah, you're right, actually, Sue! And if it had been a really comfy chair I would have probably been out straight away – and stayed asleep and missed everything. But, to be fair to me, it was about the only time I ever got any peace and quiet! It was always chaos at home, so this was my chance to have a little nap!

Sue: You were always good in the hospital, really – despite sometimes nodding off – so no, I don't think you deserved any abuse. I've no regrets about that.

Did you ever suffer from morning sickness?

Sue: It was absolutely horrendous with Chris. But there wasn't really any problem with the rest of them as regards morning sickness. I may have felt a little sick now and again, but it was nothing like I went through with Chris.

Did you ever have antenatal depression, or postnatal depression?

Sue: Yes, with James, our ninth child, I did suffer from postnatal depression, and it was quite bad. I think, partly, that was to do with Noel having had his vasectomy during that pregnancy. My postnatal depression lasted about six months. I just felt so rubbish. I had to be on antidepressants for the whole six months – but after the six months, that was it, I was fine. I think a lot of women get postnatal depression, but maybe it's something that's not talked about enough. I was fortunate, I think, because the antidepressants were really good. They got me through those six months – in fact, I would say even after just a few days of taking them, they started to work and have a positive effect.

Were the births natural, or did you have to undergo any Caesarean births?

Sue: They were all natural, I am very pleased – and grateful – to be able to say.

How different was your very first experience of giving birth to your 22nd – physically and mentally? Did it seem like the easiest, most natural thing in the world by the 22nd?

Sue: My first was absolutely horrendous. I remember having to be cut and then the midwife didn't numb me enough and I needed stitches and could feel the needle going in and the thread coming out. I can still hear the noises associated with it all. It was absolutely terrible.

Noel: It was really bad. So bad. If anyone has ever cut through bacon rind with an old pair of scissors, it was like that – that's the noise. It was just awful.

Sue: At that moment, I just thought, 'Right, that's it. I NEVER want to have any more children. I can't go through all this again.' Then I remember when I got pregnant with Sophie, I was thinking, 'Oh my God' – because it was just so traumatic the first time.

Noel: History could have been so different if we'd decided to stop after Chris because of what Sue went through – it would have been 'Sue and Noel, mum and dad of one!'

Sue: But thankfully, Sophie's birth was a lot better.

Noel: And then we never looked back!

Sue: Really, after Chris, all the births were pretty straightforward. People might assume that after having a lot of kids, it stops hurting – but it always hurts. It's never easy.

Noel: The difference is that you know what to expect, don't you?

Sue: Yes, I think, mentally, you perhaps do feel a little more relaxed after going through it all a few times. But you do still worry about the things that can go wrong, because labour and delivery can be unpredictable.

Chloe had bad colic – was this the cause of your worst sleep deprivation, or were there worse cases? And how do you cope during the days when you are sleep-deprived and lacking energy?

Sue: Chloe was the worst, in terms of sleep deprivation. As my mum used to say, 'It's a form of torture, sleep deprivation.' And that's totally right. It's so bad because you literally feel like you can't cope or function throughout the day.

  Noel: That's it – and Chloe was sleeping through the day, and so she was absolutely fine then, but there was no way you could sleep, Sue, because you had so many things to do, and I couldn't because I was at work.

  Sue: You literally just have to get on with it, don't you? But you are walking around like a zombie. Then I remember when we were expecting Jack – and we were thinking, 'Please don't have colic!' But it was just Chloe, thankfully.

With having so many kids, have you suffered with a weak bladder and had to do pelvic floor exercises to try to rectify this?

Sue: No, definitely not. I can honestly say that I can sneeze without peeing myself!

  Noel: That's always a win, isn't it?

Have you suffered with a lot of back pain over the years, associated with your pregnancies?

Sue: Yeah, definitely, I have – especially during pregnancies. I think it's sciatica – when you have shooting pains down your legs and back, and I've had those. And I've had general back pain. All in all, though, really, I think I've been lucky – I don't have a permanent bad back. I just had some back pain now and again when I was pregnant.

What would you say, in general, about the effects on your body over the years – it must have taken more punishment, and you must have suffered more in various ways, than women who have only had a few children, or maybe one or two or even none?

Sue: I don't think having all these children has had any kind of long-lasting effect on me physically. In fact, I'd probably say I am healthier than a lot of my friends who have only had a few children. I think it has all kept me younger – and a bit healthier than I might have been.

Did having so many children ever have a negative effect on your sex drive? Actually, I'm guessing not, because you often got pregnant very soon after giving birth. Was Noel ever bothered – or, er, frustrated – about the times you two weren't able to make love?

Noel: The woman who asked this has answered her own question, really! I think with having had 22 kids, there's no lack of drive there!
  Sue: Definitely not!
  Noel: No, I don't think so.
  Sue: I don't, either.
  Noel: And there's been no frustration.

Is your sex life today just the same as it ever was, or do you think it has changed a lot – not because of your age or Noel's age, but because of all the kids you have had?

Sue: I think we prefer sleep to sex now, don't we? I think when you get a bit older, you definitely appreciate your sleep a bit more.

Noel: That's right – but there's also Heidie, our youngest, to consider as well. She is a real mummy's girl and never leaves Sue alone!

What have all the pregnancies, if anything, done to the nature of your skin?

Sue: Wasn't there a survey done a while ago, saying the more children you have it's supposed to release something in your body that is meant to help your skin and make you look younger? I can't remember what it was, but I think it's definitely a thing because I've had people message me very kindly about that, saying, 'Your skin's lovely.'

There has been a study which suggests women who have had three or more children start to go through the menopause later than women who have had less than three children. You are only 48, so, I am guessing, you haven't started going through it yet. What are your feelings about this and the whole subject of the menopause?

Sue: I haven't started going though it yet, and neither have my friends who are the same age as me. One of them has had six children, but one of them has only had two – and she thinks she might be starting. It comes to every woman and so you just have to deal with it, don't you?

I had a lot of stitches on the two occasions I gave birth and had to sit on a rubber ring for a couple of days because of the pain I felt after childbirth – I can't imagine what you must have gone through having had 22 children! Were you very lucky, or did you suffer a lot of pain and damage involving your, ahem, private parts?

Sue: Like I said earlier, Chris was horrendous – I had to be cut with him and then stitched up. It took me a good six to eight weeks to get over that. I couldn't walk properly. I couldn't really sit down properly. It was absolutely horrendous. But I don't think I ever tried sitting on a rubber ring. Luckily, with the rest of them, I didn't have to have stitches.

Have your general energy levels decreased over the years? You must be absolutely knackered! I am, and I only had four kids.

Sue: Definitely, I think. And you're just getting older as well, and have so much going on. I think it all has an effect on you.

How have you approached discipline? Do you believe, for example, in having a 'naughty step'?

Sue: When we had our first two, Chris and Sophie, we were a lot stricter, and we had the naughty step and all of that. But when we had more children, that just didn't work for us anymore, and I think our children are a lot better-behaved because we're not on at them all the time, saying, 'No! Don't do this! Don't do that!'

Noel: They tend to rebel if you do that, don't they?

Sue: I think you can go overboard with the naughty step and things like that.

Noel: We try to teach them good manners; please and thank you and things like that.

Sue: And the difference between right and wrong. Also, we've found some of the older kids tend to automatically get involved in helping us police the younger ones – we don't ask them to, it just seems to be a natural thing for them to do.

Noel: Exactly – if a four-year-old and a five-year-old are arguing, you'll then hear a 12-year-old telling them, 'Don't be doing that.'

Did any of your children ever tell you NOT to have any more kids? And did any of them ENCOURAGE you to have as many as possible?

Sue: None of our kids, at any time, ever said to us that they didn't want us to have any more. Some of them have now said, 'Are you going to have any more?' – in the hope we are. But we've said, 'No, we're not.' A few of them would like us to have more, but others are not really bothered.

Do you have a babysitting rota? Is babysitting compulsory or voluntary for the older children living at home?

Sue: No, we don't have a babysitting rota. If we want to go out, one of the older ones will babysit and, quite often, they'll be the ones that say, 'Oh, I'll have the kids if you want to go out tonight.' They are pretty good like that.

Do all the kids get on, or do some split into their own little groups – or even try to go solo, not mixing with anyone?

Sue: I would say Max, our 13th child, doesn't really mix too much. He quite likes to go solo. They do mostly tend to hang around in groups.

Noel: There's Oscar and Casper who hang around together.

Sue: They're inseparable, aren't they?

Noel: Then there's Hallie and Phoebe – but then sometimes you'll see Hallie, Phoebe, Archie and Bonnie all together. It just depends on what they're doing, really.

Sue: Yeah, that's right. But all in all, they do all get on well together.

Noel: It's just natural for kids to stick together with other kids in the same sort of age group.

Did you ever feel you were running out of names that you liked when the time came to choose another one?

Sue: Yes, definitely. That happened with Heidie, our 22nd child. Bonnie, our 21st, we also struggled with. There's been a few occasions.

Noel: Who was the girl you wanted to call Aubrey? Though it would have had to have ended with an 'e' – so Aubree, I guess.

Sue: I think that was Bonnie.

Noel: There were a few discussions over that. You were set on Aubrey, or Aubree, weren't you, and I was just not having that. All I could think of was that boxer – and he wasn't even called Aubrey, but Audley... Audley Harrison.

Sue: I'm so glad you talked me out of it. I much prefer 'Bonnie.' We also had another name picked out for Heidie, but I can't think what that name was. I even had a Babygro made with the name on it, but I just can't, for the life of me, think of the name.

Noel: For Bonnie, we were going to pick from four names –

Cute kids Sue at 10 months old and Noel in primary school uniform, aged six or seven (above)

Young love This is the first photo we have of us as a couple (left) – we think we were 19 and 15 when it was taken

Brotherly love Noel, three (right), with his brother, Ian, four. 'My first memory is of me and Ian having our picture taken – sitting on a wall outside our first house'

By the seaside Sue, at 18 months old, with her brother, Stephen and their mum, Christine. 'While I was born in Bishop Auckland, Stephen was born in Liverpool'

Church bells On our wedding day *(above left)*; Noel – looking very skinny – in Gambia on our honeymoon *(above)*. Can you believe we can't find any photographs of the two of us from that romantic trip?

Like father, like son Our first born, Chris, aged four, in the garden with David, Noel's dad *(left)*

Soak up the sun Sue and Chris on holiday in Gran Canaria. 'Wow – it's hard to believe it when I look back now. Here I was, still young myself, having my first baby'

Our first daughter Sue and Sophie at Sophie's christening. 'It was so special, having my first girl – my first daughter'

A growing family Sue, Noel, Chris and Sophie. 'We had been living together – me, Sue and Chris – as a family for well over two years by the time Sophie was born'

And then there were three Sue, Noel, Chris and Sophie when Chloe was born. 'Chloe was 7lb 2oz – but to me, she was the dinkiest one, because she had really skinny legs, and long fingers'

Too cool for school Looking good in their school uniforms – *back row:* Luke and Millie; *middle:* Katie; *right middle:* James; *bottom left:* Ellie, then Josh and Aimee

Visits to gran
Left to right: Jack, Daniel, Sue's mum Christine and Sophie with Chloe at the back

Festive times
With Father Christmas at their school in 2010 – *left to right:* James, Millie, Aimee, Ellie, Luke and Katie

Hot off the press
The start of it all... nearly! Our first appearance in the media was a story in our local paper, *The Visitor*, in 2008 – we can't find that, but here is the follow-up story in the *Lancashire Evening Post*!

Down under Pointing at a sign in Australia!
Left to right: Katie, Sue, Josh, Oscar, Ellie, Aimee and Tillie with Max at the front

Radfords in Oz This was taken during our holiday in Australia in 2016 *(above)*

Gone but not forgotten We visit Alfie's grave *(right)* frequently as a family

Double celebration The christening of our two youngest children, Bonnie and Heidie, in 2021 *(below)*

Still counting
A group shot from 2017 when Sue was pregnant with Archie

Reptile fun
Holding a giant python on holiday in Australia in 2016 – *left to right:* Daniel, Jack, Chloe, Luke and James

Good as gold
A school photo from 2022 – *back row:* Casper and Oscar, *front row:* Hallie, Archie and Phoebe

Black tie At the Family Business Awards at the Titanic Hotel, Liverpool, in 2022. *Left to right:* Luke, Noel, Sue, Chloe and her partner, Jake Wallace

Proud parents We are so proud of Luke for coming out as bisexual on national television – here he is with Sue and Heidie at Lancaster Pride in 2021

A Radford family Christmas Christmases for us are just crazy, but absolutely amazing as well. They're such a special part of the year for us all because for so many years the house has just been full of so many excited children. Wrapping paper flying everywhere!

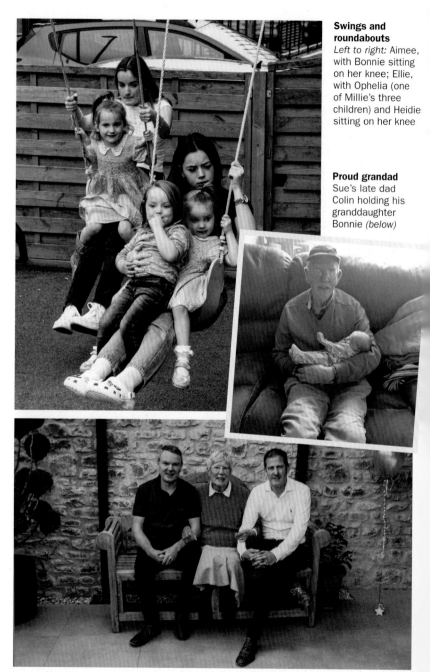

Swings and roundabouts
Left to right: Aimee, with Bonnie sitting on her knee; Ellie, with Ophelia (one of Millie's three children) and Heidie sitting on her knee

Proud grandad
Sue's late dad Colin holding his granddaughter Bonnie *(below)*

Miss you, mum Noel, his beloved late mum, Val, and his brother, Ian but you didn't want 'Heidi' on that occasion. But when you did, I said 'You can't put an 'e' on the end of 'Heidi'. But we did, eventually, even though it was my fault it was initially spelt wrong on the birth certificate!

Sue: How could you do that?!?

Parents never stop worrying about their kids – no matter how old they are. I've got four kids – two have grown-up and left home – and feel anxious about all of them. How on earth do you cope with these natural parental feelings?

Sue: There is always worry, of course, You are always going to worry about your kids whatever their age, and I think over the years we've had our fair share of worry – for example, with what happened with Tillie, and then the pregnancies after we lost Alfie. But ultimately, you've just got to try to get on with things as best you can.

Noel: With the older ones, you think they're big and old enough to look after themselves and if they want any help, they will ask for it. The main thing you worry about is their health. Our friend's daughter is poorly with cancer, and we think how lucky we have been. You know that any day it could come knocking at your door, you just don't know. But you've just got to live your lives as best you can and always be there for your kids.

Sue: You also always worry about being the best parent you can be. Maybe we're lucky in that our days can be so busy and frantic that we haven't got the time to dwell on things too much and worry.

Could there yet be baby number 23?

Sue: No, I don't think so – though we have said similar things before! But no, that's it now.

Noel: We've said similar things plenty of times before! But seriously, Heidie is three now, so yes...we're enjoying our sleep at last! And we no longer have to worry about kids being at that age when they pick things up off the floor and stick them in their mouths.

Sue: Yeah, there are all sorts of things we no longer have to worry about. But honestly, thanks to everyone who has been interested enough to ask me a question over the years.

Noel: Yes, thank you – they weren't too painful, were they, Sue?

Sue: I really don't mind being asked questions. Me and Noel appreciate the fact that people are interested in our family. I hope I've been able to give other women a bit of a flavour of my own life as a mum – and men, too, of course!

Chapter 16

Home truths

Sue on Noel

I think I'm going to enjoy this part of the chapter – because it's my chance to talk about Noel! Ah, there's so much to say! But don't worry, Noel, it's going to be MOSTLY good. How could it not be?

Seriously, though, I still really fancy Noel – he's still got it! And it's not just one thing I fancy or love about him – it's the whole package. I could never imagine ever being with anyone else. In fact, I think we're more in love now than when we first got together. I see a bit of Tom Cruise in Noel – although one of the kids did say they saw a bit of Ian Beale (Adam Woodyatt) from EastEnders! Noel's also been compared to Steven Gerrard – but no, I just see Tom Cruise!

A lot of people do think that because we've got so many children and we've got so much going on in our lives that we no longer have any time for each other, but our relationship and our marriage shows me and Noel definitely do. And even though we started off with Chris very young and a lot of people thought we'd never last, we've shown how strong our relationship has always been.

One of the most important things in a relationship is being friends – and me and Noel are great friends. I think you have to be best friends with your partner at the end of the day – and Noel is definitely my best friend.

And I'm pleased to say he's very much a man for romantic gestures. He'll come home from work with a bunch of flowers, or a box of chocolates. He's always been romantic.

Noel is quite a laid-back kind of person who doesn't let things get to him. He's a very hard worker – he began working, doing odd jobs like delivering milk, when he was 12. This has been a great thing for the family as a whole, because Noel has instilled that into the kids. They know that hard work is important, thanks to Noel.

He's also quite a good listener – well, mostly. Sometimes, you can be telling him something and he can be quite quiet as if he's not taking it in – and I don't think he is on those occasions!

He's very good with the kids. He's always the one who, if I'm stressing out about something, will be like, 'It'll all be fine, you just need to take a step back.' He's the kind of person who will help keep me grounded and from stressing out too much. Noel's such a dependable person.

He's also the one who doesn't always spend a lot, and keeps his wallet very firmly closed! I'm laughing but I think that can be quite a good quality – he's sensible with money and more conscious when it comes to spending, whereas I'm not so much like that!

I think Noel is a lot more relaxed these days, compared to when he was much younger. He's very calm now. When we first had our business, I'd say he was more stressed. He's mellowed with age!

I think that me and Noel have a really good relationship; we're definitely soulmates. Sometimes I'll be thinking something and Noel will immediately say exactly what I was about to say – it's so weird. We also finish each other's sentences.

I also feel a bit lost when he's not around for any length of time. And I know Noel's the same.

He's got a wicked sense of humour – his one-liners are just first-class. He can be so funny – very similar to my late dad in his sense of humour and personality. His cooking is also amazing. He is so good at being able to rustle something up when there isn't much in, just before a big shop – he'll open a cupboard and make a fantastic meal out of whatever he finds. I think that comes from being a chef when he was younger.

He does drive me crazy when he bites his nails, though. It's so bad, and so noisy – I hate it. And when he leaves his dirty clothes in the bathroom – that is also really annoying. Sometimes he's so bad at putting things down and forgetting where he's put them. That's when I think he's like my 23rd child! As he's getting older, I don't think his memory is quite what it was!

Noel on Sue

I was biting my fingernails when you were giving your opinions on me, Sue! No, I think I got off lightly there – and now it's my turn! But I don't think you've got too much to worry about, either.

I do quite often sit there and look at Sue, when she doesn't know I'm looking at her, and think to myself, 'What a great-looking woman she is.'

Somebody said to us when we were on our honeymoon that Sue reminded them of Demi Moore – I totally agreed, and Sue loved the comparison, too. I'd still go along with that, and still think we're on our honeymoon!

Sue is the whole package for me but if I did have to pick one part of her – she does have lovely legs. They're not very long legs, but they're lovely! She's always had really good legs – when she was younger, she was a swimmer and a gymnast. I always knew Sue was the one, from the very start. I'm that type of person – very committed. And I fought hard for us to stay together as a family – and Sue did, too. Our date nights are really important to us. We try to let our hair down and have a really good catch-up. Sue likes to be romanced, rather than be the romantic one. I think she enjoys me giving her flowers and chocolates. Maybe this is the way it should be – to be honest, it would feel a bit odd if I came home from work to find a bunch of flowers on the table from Sue and a nice romantic meal being prepared! Sue is a very caring person – she always puts everyone else before herself, especially the kids and myself. Sue's not happy until everyone else is happy.

She's not a negative person, she doesn't see the bad in people. And if someone has been horrible to her in the past, she will still see the positive in that person – she doesn't hold grudges.

With the kids, she always wants to please them. It's important to her to give them the best life she possibly can. She just wants them to always be happy. There's no one more caring than Sue.

And if Sue wasn't here, I think the house would just go to pot. The only thing I think I contribute around the house is the cooking. The cleaning, all the washing and any general housework is all down to Sue. And there's a lot of cleaning and washing needed in this house! If that wasn't all done, I'd be totally lost to be honest. Also, Sue's the one who will organise things for the family – days out, holidays, whatever. She is such a great organiser. She is the diary of the house.

I wouldn't say Sue is outgoing. She's quite a shy person. If she was going to try something new, I think it would have to involve me. She wouldn't want to go on her own.

But I think I'm like that as well. Though once Sue gets to know people, she's a right good laugh. Sue's not the greatest comedian, but she likes having a laugh and she's quite happy to take the mick out of me!

Overall, I think she's definitely more chilled than she was years ago. I think I am, too. When you've had your first child you just worry about everything. 'Should they be doing this? Should they be doing that?' Now, it's more an attitude of, 'It's OK, it'll be fine. Just carry on with life.'

Like Sue, I do find it weird that we always seem to know what the other is thinking about. One of us will say something and the other will say, 'I was just thinking that.' And if Sue is ever away, I do miss her – pine for her, really. She once went to New York with the girls and it was OK for the first day or two, but then I just hated it. She was only away for four nights.

I do enjoy cooking, but if Sue could cook, too, that would be great. There are some days that's all I do at work, as well, and I can then come home to cook tea for everyone, and I'm tired and think, 'I just can't be bothered.' Sue will pick up on it on those days and she will make something for tea that night – and there are things she can do. But, to be honest, Sue's cooking is generally out of a jar or a bag or packet!

I think, of the two of us, it's my outlook that's changed in recent years. I've been the more cautious one, while Sue might say, 'Let's spend this now or do that now' and I'll be saying, 'Let's hold back a bit and maybe do that in a few years' time.' But I usually just go along with Sue!

Her annoying habits are putting my stuff away and then, when I can't find whatever it is that I'm looking for, she blames me! But she does tidy up a lot so she's always putting things away, whereas, and it's maybe a typical fella thing, I'll think, 'I'll leave that there so I know where it is.' Then Sue comes along, tidies it away and I no longer know where it is!

Chapter 17

Nine pets – and counting?

Noel: Oh dear, I can hear people shouting at their books and their Kindles… 'What!?! They've got seven dogs and two rabbits in the house as well as all those kids? I don't believe it!' Yes, guilty as charged. Er, Sue, help me out here…

Sue: Yes, we do realise it must seem strange that, as well as having so many kids, we have also decided to have all these pets. I know there will be people who have one dog and think that is hard work, and so they would never get a second one (let alone a third, fourth, fifth, sixth and seventh!). What can we say? We just love dogs and both grew up with them – and we've always had dogs ourselves. Don't get me wrong – sometimes it can be absolutely crazy when you've got people round, and the dogs are all barking. But no, we wouldn't be without them. We love them and they're a part of the family.

Noel: I suppose we could also make the argument that, having had 22 kids, things couldn't really be any more chaotic – so why not add seven dogs into the mix? And actually, sometimes, because of all the kids, some visitors don't even notice the dogs that much! But Sue's right, we've always loved having dogs around. When we got our first house, we got a dog – a mongrel dog, a bit of a Heinz 57. He was lovely – and, as the years went by, we got back into them and got a few more. And to be honest, the dogs don't make as much mess as the kids! They don't leave things scattered all over the house like the kids do, day in and day out. But we must admit, the dogs do demand more attention!

Sue: As they are very much part of the Radford family, let us introduce you to them… Lola the collie is nine-years-old.

Bluebell and Ivy are French bulldogs and both five.

Mabel, our third French bulldog, is four.

Cookie and Minnie are Mini-Dachshunds and both two years old.

Dolly, our third Mini-Dachshund, is one.

And we've had them all since they were puppies.

You'll notice Lola is our only collie, so you might think she's a bit out on her own – and you'd be absolutely right! The Frenchies tend to stick around together, while the Dachshunds will stay with each other, as well. Lola doesn't like to associate with any of the other dogs – the Frenchies or the Dachshunds – so she stays out of their way.

Noel: She'll spend all her time with the girls.

Sue: Not quite all her time – do you remember, Noel, when we were doing that photo shoot in the garden, and Lola was humping the kids' toys?

Noel: How could I forget? That's an image that will stay with me for a long time!

Sue: Lola's the oldest and, generally speaking, I don't think she can be bothered with the noise made by the other, younger dogs, or their hyperactivity. I think she probably felt a bit invaded when we got the others – she would have been quite happy to have been the only dog in the house.

We got the Frenchies and the Dachshunds because we think those breeds are so, so lovable. They are so good with the kids, too. But so is Lola, to be fair. I think the younger kids prefer the Dachshunds, though, because they are so small.

Noel: The occasional humping of kids' toys aside, Lola is so placid. The kids can be jumping all over her, and she won't be at all bothered. She just doesn't care.

Sue: Lola is so funny. We'll give her loads of attention because she loves that, and if she's not ready for you to stop stroking her she'll certainly let you know about it – she'll paw you until you start stroking her again!

Anyway, yes, we do accept that it may seem like a lot of dogs in one house. They obviously do involve extra work for us – Lola, for example, is a terrible shedder. But, fortunately, the Frenchies and the Dachshunds don't tend to shed too much, so we don't have to brush up after them all the time like we do with Lola. As for vets' bills, which I know are a big worry for everyone who has pets, all of our dogs are in good health – apart from Ivy, who is on permanent medication for her bad skin. But the rest of them are fine, so we count our blessings regarding that, as it's just their annual boosters that cost us money at the vets. But they do all like different food, so they're not on the same thing – which would make things easier for us.

Noel: A lot of dogs are more than happy to eat some of what their owners eat. But Lola can be a bit fussy – she won't eat a lot of the things we do. Ivy – if it's not nailed down, she'll eat it, while the rest of them can also be quite picky.

The kids don't really take ownership of certain dogs or have their favourites; they'll just cuddle whichever dog is around. They get on with them all and love playing with them. And when we go away for weekend breaks and holidays, the older ones who stay behind will be the ones who look after the dogs – so it's good to have our own dog minders on tap! There have been some occasions when we've been out with a lot of the kids and, I'd say, four of the dogs – and it's been a bit chaotic to say the least.

Sue: We don't tend to walk all the dogs at the same time, because it would just be too much. I don't think it would be safe. The maximum we would take out at one time is four, but then you have to make sure there are a few of us with them so they'll be fully under control. And who does the walking will just depend on what we've all got on from day to day. They go for their walks in the evenings, and it will be a mix of me and the older kids who take them out.

Noel: To be honest, the Dachshunds are not too interested in going out at all. They need to be dragged out – they're a bit lazy, to say the least.

Sue: All the dogs have their own personalities, I suppose. Bluebell, one of the Frenchies, certainly went through a phase where she kept us on our toes. For a while, she didn't have such a good temperament and didn't like to be around other dogs, and we got a dog trainer involved – which viewers might remember from series two. It worked, and now she's really good around other dogs.

So, yes, 22 kids and seven dogs – but let's not forget about the rabbits! Peter and Oreo are both two. They're lop-eared rabbits and live outside – they're Aimee's rabbits and she adores them. But although they have their hutch outside, they do sometimes come into the house – into the living room and upstairs, as well. They're mostly outside, but when they do come into the house, we have to make sure the dogs are kept away from them.

Noel: The rabbits are lovely little things, and pretty low maintenance compared to the dogs – and the kids!

I think we'll stop at seven dogs and two rabbits – I think nine pets is plenty, though Tillie did ask not so long ago for a tortoise. I had one as a kid and he was called Humphrey. They don't do much, though, do they? They certainly don't move much. Actually, that's an argument in favour of getting one!

Chapter 18

Not just a Mum and Dad... This is us!

Sue: It's not really surprising that many people will simply view me as a mum, albeit one of 22 kids! We're all defined by something, and I'm more than happy to be seen as 'That woman who has all those children.' I'm really proud of being a mum, as well as a wife and a grandmother. Family is everything to me and Noel but, like everybody else, we are obviously individuals as well. Here's just a little bit about me, then – and I'll do my best not to mention the kids and Noel too much!

* * *

Some people might not believe it, but I've never been to a music concert in my life. That, though, is about to change – finally! I'm a Taylor Swift girl. I just love ALL her music – and all my older daughters love her, too. Me, Chloe, Ellie and Aimee are all set to see her in concert in Liverpool as part of her Eras Tour 2024. It's going to be so nice, because it's something we can do together. There's no one else for me in the music world – it's all about Taylor Swift! We've already talked about what we'll wear on the big night and it's going to be such an exciting occasion for us all.

I've not got any old vinyl records or any CDs – I've just never had the time. I don't listen to the radio much, either. I will hear music via Amazon, maybe, and the kids would have probably played me something by Taylor Swift one day, and that's how I would have first got into her music.

I do know I really can't be doing with rapping stuff – that kind of music drives me mad. I hate it. If any of the boys have got some rap on, I'm just... 'Oh no, please!' I can't stand it. I can't listen to it.

I love watching *Coronation Street* and *Emmerdale*, which drives Noel crazy because he just does not like soaps at all. Sometimes I'll watch *EastEnders* but I'm not really a massive fan. I also love to watch the old episodes of *Benidorm* – it's so funny.

I also like programmes such as *Police Interceptors* and *24 Hours in A&E* – those real-life shows are fascinating. And I can sit there and watch a reality TV programme now – having been involved in them myself for a good while – and think, 'Oh yeah, I know how they've done that.'

Who's that guy I cannot abide who had that morning programme on the TV? Oh yes, Matthew Wright on *The Wright Stuff*. I couldn't stand watching him. Ugh! He just grates on me for some reason. But now, if I ever get the chance during the day, I would sit down and watch *Loose Women* – I do love that programme. And I might be able to watch a little bit of *This Morning*, but besides that I don't really get the chance to watch anything during the day.

With movies, I'm not a fan of those all-action, 'Shooty Shooty Bang Bang' type films that Noel enjoys. I love comedy films like *Bridesmaids* and *Step Brothers* – anything like that is really funny.

I never read any books, or even newspapers or magazines, because I just don't get the chance. It would be lovely to be able to go on holiday, sit on a sun lounger and just read. But neither of us get a chance to do that.

It's great when we get the chance to go out to a restaurant. My dream three-course meal would start with a lovely homemade soup – something like potato and leek or vegetable – with a nice crusty roll. Then I would have a steak, with mash and some long-stemmed broccoli and asparagus, and finish off with chocolate cake and cream. All with a glass of Prosecco!

We recently had a Baby Guinness (coffee liqueur topped by a layer of Irish cream) for the first time – and were like, 'Oh wow, these are amazing!' It was while we were out filming, and we said, 'Why have we never had one of these before?' And I like pink gin and lemonade, too.

I love Doritos and dips – especially if I'm just sitting and relaxing in the evening, watching the telly. You can't beat that.

I can't stand sprouts. Once I remember my mum and dad put sprouts on my plate when I was a kid and I was made to eat them. They were absolutely disgusting and I just remember being sick into this stainless-steel tumbler type thing and I just thought, 'Never, ever again!' Noel's a great cook and he's tried it all in a bid to make them more appealing to me – sprouts with chestnuts and with bacon and with almonds – but no, I was scarred for life at an early age!

My dream day out, without the kids, would be just meeting up with friends and going out for lunch. It's so difficult to balance a busy family life with your friends, because obviously we're all busy. But we do all try to make an effort to meet up once in a while and go for something to eat.

It would also be lovely to have a nice spa day – including a nice massage, because I feel that lugging all that washing up and down the stairs every day for so many years has taken its toll on my joints.

I don't like football, I hate cricket, and I don't watch tennis – I find it quite boring. But I do quite like swimming – I've done open water swimming in Lake Windermere and would like to carry on doing that because it's quite therapeutic. I will sit and watch sport on the telly, but I wouldn't make a point of putting it on. I think I'd rather be taking part in something – like doing the open water swimming – rather than watching other people.

With football, my team has to be Liverpool – I wouldn't dare support anyone else, because Noel and the older kids who are interested all support Liverpool. My dad, who's passed away now, was a really big Liverpool fan for years, and then they started losing during a really bad season, sometime in the 1990s, and he just switched like that – to supporting, of all teams, Manchester United! Because they were winning at the time. Who does that? He wasn't bothered at all; he had no shame about it. He just loved Alex Ferguson and he never switched back to Liverpool. That was just my dad – he was an absolute comedian, and just didn't care.

My bugbear in life is rude people – I just can't be doing with them. Why do some people have to be rude and nasty? There's no need for it and it really annoys me.

Me and Noel are very much the same. We're not rude people and we just end up kind of taking it when people are rude to us. And it really annoys me because if someone is being rude to me,

.I will just stand there and accept it because of the sort of person I am. Then you think, 'Why didn't I say something back?' But we're both the same – we just roll with things and we don't like confrontations.

I don't follow politics and I'm not really interested at all. I was never really brought up with it; my mum and dad didn't seem interested. But they were always Labour people – they said that they were for the working people and the Conservatives were more for the upper class. We're probably more Labour ourselves.

As for religion, we're both Church of England. We don't go to church. I used to go to Sunday School when I was younger and the kids have all been christened but we're not religious church-goers.

If I was asked to describe myself, I'd say I'm quite a sensitive person. But I'm quite laid-back, I don't tend to let things get to me very much. I like to make sure everyone is happy around me. I don't like confrontation. I'm quite a shy person, really. I think a lot of people think that because you're on telly then you must be an outgoing person, but me and Noel are both quite shy. We like to keep ourselves to ourselves.

Noel: Sue is right – we can't complain if people just view us as being a mum and dad. We're delighted to be the parents of 22 children, and that's what will always be the most important thing in our lives. We love being at the head of a big family and we don't get a lot of time to do anything that doesn't involve the kids. Again, we wouldn't complain about that – because we chose to have a big family and we love what it gives us. We wouldn't want things to be any different. Right, then, I suppose I'd better say a bit about me – and no doubt there is bound to be something in the following that the kids will pick up on and take the mickey out of me about!

* * *

I like all sorts of music. My main thing is rock music – I love AC/DC. U2 – I'm an absolute fan of them and always have been.

Mumford & Sons were my favourite group for quite a while. Anything like that, I like. Eighties music I really love. Round here, when some of the older kids are sitting in the kitchen in the evening, I'll end up being the DJ, with Amazon or YouTube, and it's generally all the 80s tunes that I'll put on. And the older kids all like the 80s tunes – they're all so catchy and accessible – though I don't play so much of the cheesy pop stuff.

I think my interest in music all stems from my older brother, Ian. He got me into listening to the charts, and we'd listen to them on the Sunday evening – the top 40 rundown. He'd always buy what was number one. He had the big record collection and I'd get to listen to it. My record collection amounted to two singles – one was the Band Aid, *Do They Know It's Christmas?* one, which I got when it came out in 1984, while the first single I bought, the year before, was Ozzy Osbourne's *Bark At The Moon*. That was probably quite a fitting song, thinking about the fact I went on to have 22 kids!

And the first album I bought was *Prince Charming* by Adam and the Ants. I fell out with my mum one day so I scratched it – instead of scratching one of her records! I somehow believed I was better off scratching my only album. I don't know what I was thinking there. It was a strange act of self-harm when I think about it now!

Though me and Sue have never been to any concerts together, and Sue hasn't been to any at all, I have been to one. For my Christmas present a few years ago, Sue kindly bought me a ticket to go and see Mumford & Sons. So myself and Chloe went to watch them in Manchester, and it was a great night. Not going to concerts never bothered me when I was younger. Sue's brother Stephen used to go to see all the heavy metal bands play at the festivals in Donington Park, but I've never felt I've missed out regarding concerts. I don't think either of us have. But actually, I did want to go and see AC/DC once up in Glasgow, but I never got round to it.

I'm more of a film person than a fan of TV programmes. It doesn't matter when it is, I'm more than happy to sit down and watch a good film. I can watch a film more than once, to be honest, which might sound a bit bizarre. But in this house, if you want to watch something, the amount of chatter over the top of it can mean you miss things the first time round anyway. But yes, regarding the types of films, Sue will say things like, 'Why are you putting a Shooty Shooty Bang Bang film on?' Films like *Saving Private Ryan* and *Full Metal Jacket* are right up my street, while I was really into Bruce Lee films when I was young. I also love thrillers and spy films. *Bridge of Spies* was a really good film. I will watch anything. I like comedy, but I'm not really a fan of romantic films – so I suppose there are things I wouldn't watch. On the telly, when it comes to comedies, the old ones are the best – I love *Only Fools and Horses*, *It Ain't Half Hot, Mum* and *Fawlty Towers*. I can't really think of newer things that I've really liked and found funny – maybe *2point4 Children*. Then again, I've never seen things like *The Office*. This is what it's like – because of our busy lives, there are so many things that have passed me by. I've never seen a single episode of *Friends*, for example. I started getting into *The Walking Dead* series, watching it with Chloe – then we forgot where we were up to and gave up on it! Generally, we won't put something on Netflix which is a series because we know we're not going to be able to keep up with it or watch the next series – or even the next episode!

I'm really not into soaps. I mean, *EastEnders*! I call it Doom and Gloom because it just seems to be miserable all the time. *Coronation Street* is alright, but I just think, 'This is a bit far-fetched.'

Me and Sue have been to the cinema together on a few occasions, though we haven't done so for a while. We try to have a date night once a month and quite often that might be going for a meal, but we have been to the cinema now and again. I remember we went to watch a James Bond film with Pierce Brosnan in donkeys' years ago in Ambleside in the Lake District – but we fell asleep! We've seen *1917*, and we've also seen a Bond film with the best Bond ever in it, Daniel Craig – and we didn't fall asleep that time!

A book popped up on my Facebook timeline recently – and I asked Sue, 'When do you think it was that I bought this book?' She said five years ago and, incredibly, it was – I'd thought it was about 18 months or two years ago, tops. It was *I Spy* by Tom Marcus. He was an MI5 agent and it was just so interesting. But I've not had the chance to read a book since then – and I just can't believe it's been five years. The book I read previous to that was *Bravo Two Zero* by Andy McNab – and it's probably 20 years since I read that!

The last time I really had the chance to read a newspaper was years ago when we went to Sue's parents for Sunday dinner, and Sue's dad would have bought the *Sunday Mail*. The kids would be there talking to their nanna and grandad and I was thinking, 'I can sit and read the magazine bit in the paper' – a real luxury!

For my dream meal, I would start with garlic mushrooms with balsamic vinegar and some nice bread to dip in it. I'd then have a steak with dauphinoise potatoes, and any other vegetables would do me – I just love vegetables. And then sticky toffee pudding – with both ice cream and cream!

Chocolate is my comfort food. I absolutely love it. Cadbury's is my favourite. Foods I DON'T like – liver and onions! Who likes liver and onions? Or kidneys? Weird. As a kid, though, I remember my mum was able to get me to eat lambs' hearts and sheep's brains. I'm not even sure you can get them now. It wasn't every day, just now and again – thankfully!

Drink-wise – around the house I'll just have a bottle of beer, a bottle of lager. If I was out and about, on the lash, I imagine it would start off with a lager, but my favourite drink – although some of my friends would say it's a bit dangerous because you can end up in a bit of a mess after it – is vodka Martini with lemonade. It's a really nice drink, but you can only have one or two.

The ideal day, if the kids weren't involved, would be to be able to get out somewhere with Sue to have some lunch, and have a look around – whether it be a little town or whatever, just to take some time and maybe do a bit of shopping. Just to spend that time together, just the two of us.

My main friend, Jamie, lives in Edinburgh so we don't really get the chance to go out together too often, and I'm probably a bit too old to be going out on the lash now! But I do like doing things as an individual – I went clay pigeon shooting once and absolutely loved that, and I recently started flying lessons in the hope I can get my pilot's licence. That's been an ambition of mine for a good while.

With the motorhome, we've been to Devon and Cornwall and love both those places. Scotland was good, and there are still plenty of places in the UK we would like to explore. And that is our long-term plan, when the kids are older – me and Sue will then be able to venture off into the sunset together!

When I lived in Kendal, my mum and dad were not into sport at all, but my next-door neighbour supported Liverpool and he took me to a match in 1978, when I was just seven, and that was it. Obviously, I'm a Liverpool supporter because that's what I've been since I was seven but, if I'm being honest, I could probably only name one of their players today. I just don't follow it so much now, but I will support them when they come on the telly. It's the older boys who keep it going in this house with Liverpool. All the older girls support Liverpool, too.

I can watch pretty much all sports apart from snooker and cricket. I just don't understand cricket. I don't understand how they can have different scores and yet it's still a draw. But golf I can watch, some athletics and Rugby Union I love – the Six Nations. Rugby League just seems a bit boring – piling on top of each other, and then they have to get off and pass the ball. I like it when they're kicking the hell out of each other in Rugby Union!

I used to run a lot in my 20s – and before that, I did cross country running for the school. Then, after leaving school, I got into fell-running. I've done a couple of marathons and half-marathons. But I've not done anything for a while – I think fell-running knackered up one of my knees.

What DON'T I like? Internet trolls, ha ha! I can't stand rude people, and one of the worst experiences I had was when we were checking-in at the airport and showing all our passports. There were, say, 18 of us on this occasion. We put all the passports together and I remember this one guy, who was so rude, saying, 'I'm not doing all of them! Someone's going to have to come and help me.' I looked behind me and there were another 150 people queuing up and I thought, 'You've still got all of them to do after our 18.'

Politics isn't a big thing for me at all. When I was growing up it was very private, you just didn't talk about politics. I never knew who my mum or dad voted for. The only politician I can think of off the top of my head – and who I don't like – is David Cameron. He just seems creepy and untrustworthy. But, to be honest, are any of them trustworthy? You did hear a bit about politics growing up – that Labour are the ones who look after people at work while the Conservatives ... oh, I've just remembered, I hate Jacob Rees-Mogg! When posh people speak, I usually like it. But him... I absolutely hate him; he's horrible. He gives the impression he's thinking, 'I'm rich – you're not.' What bothers me in politics is when they're making decisions which end up taking money off people, and they'll say, 'We're only taking £10 off you' – but for some people, that's their electricity for the week or their gas for the week, and I don't think some of these politicians understand what £10 means to some people. Should billionaires be running the country? Shouldn't it be people who understand what the man and woman in the street are going through?

As a person, I'm like Sue. I'm quite chilled and relaxed. I'm quite outgoing and happy to try new things but, at the same time, I'm also very shy. It can be difficult when people come up to us in the street and talk to us. We do enjoy it because we like meeting people, but because we're both shy we just don't know what to say. We went to London once and we saw Rick Stein, who we love, and I was dying to say 'Hello' – but I was just too shy. We both regretted not going up to him.

Chapter 19

Our birth parents and our differing views about them

Noel: This is not a subject I find it easy to talk about – as Sue has said, this is probably because I'm a typical man! Viewers of *Britain's Biggest Family* will have seen me finding it difficult – but I think that's because it is a very private matter.

My birth mum is still none the wiser that I have been looking to find out more information about her, unless she watches us on the TV and she's maybe put two and two together. I don't think she would have been told details about who adopted me, where they were from and what my surname was going to be. I think things are completely different now compared with the time I was adopted. I could be wrong but I think that in the 1970s after you were given up, that was it. Though there may have been a six-week cooling off period, where you could change your mind and have the child back – but then there was no going back after that. I was born on Christmas Eve, 1970, and adopted on January 3, 1971 – but I don't think I was officially registered as having been adopted until March of that year.

Nothing has really happened since I was first filmed in my birthplace of Stockport for the 2023 series. And I'm still umming and ahhing about what to do. But I think I know, really – I want to get my adoption file and look at that. I already knew, before filming for the 2023 series, the name of my birth mum – because my late mum had told me. And I know some people might have thought, when they watched the last episode of the 2023 series – and the scene at the end which was a trailer for the 2024 series – that I was about to knock on my birth mum's door, but that wasn't the case. I'm still no nearer to doing so, through my own choice. The only real development for the fourth series – the 2024 series – is me going back to Stockport and looking for my adoption file. I still don't know what's in it. But I think if you were adopted just 10 or even 20 years ago, there would probably be a lot more in such a file than there would be in mine. If I was keen, I'm sure Channel 5 would want to film me going to knock on my birth mum's door – but, to be honest, I don't think I'd be into that at all. And she might be the same.

I think just getting my adoption file will be fine, because there's only me, Sue and the kids who know about that, whereas if you start involving your birth mum then it opens a can of worms, doesn't it? And I'm not ready yet to meet another family. If you've got half-brothers and half-sisters... I wouldn't be ready for that. The chances of me ever ending up knocking on my birth mum's door are probably very slim. You just don't know what would be waiting for you. But also, if I was to go looking for her, find her and she didn't want to see me, it wouldn't bother me at all. For some people, that would be a second rejection and it might get to them – but it really wouldn't bother me. Sue's the same – the people we call our mums and dads, they are our parents. Now and again I thought about trying to find out more about my birth parents, but I didn't look into it properly until recently. Maybe it was down to age – I'm getting on a bit, myself, and then I thought about my birth mum and how old she would be – she's 16 years older than me. You just think, are you running out of time? My birth mum could have been dead and buried donkeys' years ago, you just don't know.

The other thing is the health side, because when you're filling in forms and you're asked if your family has got any history of certain illnesses – well, we just don't know, but to get some knowledge of that medical history I'd have to end up knocking on my birth mum's door.

Also, my late mum always said that if I was going to find my birth mum (and if she was alive today, she would be helping me), then don't do it on TV. It is a really private thing, so I've got what my mum said, and the fact that it is such a personal thing, at the back of my mind. I have said in the past that just a photograph would be nice, but actually meeting up and then having another family... I don't know about that. If I wasn't on the telly, things might be different. If there are half-brothers and half-sisters I have no idea what they could be like – and they might say, 'Ooh, you're on the telly' and they will suddenly want to be all friendly, just because you're on the telly. It could all be a bit odd, and a bit stressful – it could even end up with all kinds of distant relations from all over the world getting in touch.

If I did ever meet my birth mum, I'd obviously be curious about what she could tell me about my birth dad. I do know more than has been on the telly. I know my dad's name as well.

I'm not really sure why I was given up for adoption. I know they made a go of it, but it just didn't work out for whatever reason. And my birth mum was very young – only 16. Whatever I do, my dad – my adoptive dad, who I see as my real dad – will always be at the forefront of my mind, because of the love and respect I have for him. But he's been supportive of my search for more information, and I know he wouldn't be bothered if I took it further. My mum and dad were always open about the fact that I was adopted – anything I would have wanted to know; they would have told me. But I never did want to know anything, so I never asked.

If I did take things further, maybe it would be better for my dad if I did it privately. And the TV people have always said that if I wanted to track down my mum privately, that is absolutely fine. I've not been pressured in any way. But I haven't spent a lot of time over the years wondering about my birth parents. Because my birthday is on Christmas Eve, then perhaps at Christmas time I have wondered if they're thinking of me. Sometimes you do think about them, but then maybe a year will go by without you thinking about them at all.

A lot of amateur psychologists may think the reason me and Sue have had lots of kids must be linked to the fact we were both adopted, but I don't think there is any connection. Unless someone comes along and sticks some electrodes on our heads, and says after doing some tests, 'Oh, this is why you've got so many kids' we're just not going to believe any of those theories.

And I never talk about any of this with our kids. It's not a taboo subject, it's just something we never talk about. I think if we did have a discussion with them all – those old enough to understand it anyway – they would all be behind me and what I've done up to this point. But I'm not interested in going the whole way – I just want to be nosey, really, and see what's in my files. I think I have to apply for my full birth certificate, and then something happens from there. I've just never got round to it! If I did end up tracking my birth mum down and she realised she had all these grandchildren – well, if she had any sense, she'd turn around and run away. 'Stuff that! I'm not getting all your kids birthday and Christmas presents!'

But on the medical history side of things, it is wrong that we don't know our family medical history – there should be some information available to us. Yes, it's just about being nosey. I'd be curious to see what's in my files – is there a letter in there from either my birth mum or dad? And it would be nice to see a photograph – but I'm pretty sure I won't be knocking on anyone's door.

Sue: I know a lot of people get to the point where they want to find out more about their birth parents, and maybe meet them, but it's just not something that I have any interest in. My brother Stephen was also adopted – and he has never been interested in getting more information about his own birth parents, either. While I was born in Bishop Auckland, Stephen was born in Liverpool. I remember when he turned 16, his birth mum tried to get in contact with him and arrange to see him – he was told this by our adoptive mum – and he just said, 'No, I'm not interested.' I've never really had anyone ask me about why I've not tried to find my birth parents. Maybe they know it's just something I've never been interested in.

I really have no feelings either way about my birth mum, though I do remember after me and Noel had our first few children – then I thought, 'Gosh, I could never have given my children up.' It's just not something I could have done, but obviously people's circumstances can be very different. And back then, in the 1970s, things were very different. Me and my brother just feel incredibly grateful that we were adopted by our parents, because we had the best upbringing and life we could possibly have had. And I know Noel feels the same way – he is glad he was adopted, too.

As for the idea that me and Noel having a lot of children is somehow connected to the fact we were both adopted – well, that's just not something we ever thought about. No, there is nothing in that – because I don't even think about my birth parents. I don't give the fact that I was adopted any thought at all, and never have. And I can't see me ever changing my mind regarding trying to find out about my birth parents.

But I have always found it very strange that you can give a child away and not have to give any family medical history and information to the authorities – so that child would know about it in their later lives. Me and Noel just don't have that knowledge about the medical history of our birth families. Thankfully, we've been really, really lucky with our children and their health. With Noel, and the search he has been on for more information, it's just up to him – you can't make a decision for someone else. I want him to realise, though, that it's not always the happy ending you want it to be. You've got to be mentally OK to take whatever it is that you find out.

As for our birth parents themselves, I would definitely think Noel's birth parents – if they are still alive, and if they watch the programme – will have a good idea about him, especially as he has been filmed in Stockport, and has said he was born on Christmas Eve, 1970.

Chapter 20

Putting our critics straight

Noel: We have certainly learned a lot about people since we started appearing on television, way back in 2012. Some of it has been great but some of it, unfortunately, not so great. We get so many lovely comments from viewers who enjoy seeing what our family is up to. They might watch us on *Britain's Biggest Family: 22 Kids and Counting*, they might watch some of the videos we put on our YouTube and TikTok channels – or they might look at the posts on our Facebook and Instagram pages.

Our own social media accounts are a nice place to be – but then there's a whole other world which, sadly, isn't quite the same. Although I guess we could now class ourselves as experts on internet trolls, we've never met any of them – probably because they spend their lives hiding behind their computers with their fake names! It's something we had to get used to pretty quickly

– and it's something we have now learned to ignore as much as we possibly can.

We don't have Twitter – or X as it's called these days. We got rid of that years ago. That's the worst of them all – it's absolutely vile. We have a Facebook page for the family and we monitor that. We find if someone does put something negative about us on there, people that do like us will jump back at them. Someone put something on about us a while back, and people really laid into them. I can't remember what it was, but it became a situation where those people who were defending us were basically saying, 'I'm going to let you have some of your own medicine, see how you like it.' But it can get a bit heated from time to time, so we delete it when things get like that. And we're also on Instagram, YouTube and TikTok.

Sue: Noel is right – Twitter, or X, is just toxic. We try to manage our own social media accounts and ignore the comments that people make elsewhere. We're really good with our social media – we very rarely get nasty and negative comments; on the whole, it's really positive. You'll get messages which are just so lovely. I think we learned a good few years ago not to go looking for the negative stuff, because it's never good for your mental health. You've really got to just try to avoid it as best you can. Because even though you get all these lovely comments, one really horrible remark can, in your mind, take over everything else.

Noel: We now just look at the comments on our own social media accounts. We don't go to newspaper sites and read the comments their readers put on – we learned not to do that a long time ago. I think some of these people say what they say just because they are sitting behind a keyboard. They think they can say anything they like and it doesn't matter – it doesn't have any consequences.

Sue: It's as if they don't really see you – the target of their abuse – as being a human being who has feelings. They don't seem to see you as a real person. They're not bothered about what they say or what effects it might have.

Noel: And quite often they are just hiding behind fake names, or no names at all – which is pretty cowardly, isn't it? But it's not just us they're doing it to. They'll have a go at us, then they'll move onto someone else. They must have such empty lives.

Sue: They can't be happy with their own lives to do what they do – to feel they need to try to drag other people down. It's sad because me and Noel are not those kinds of people. But some people, sadly, are just not very nice. To say the least!

Noel: There are people who are jealous of what you've got. And some of the media love to concentrate on the negative. For example, when we do a Q&A on Instagram if we get, say, 99 positive comments and one negative one, it will be the negative one that is picked out by a news outlet. They'll then write about how 'People are saying this about the Radfords' – when it's really just one person. Then that will snowball after being copied by other newspaper websites. The story, such as it is, seems to go everywhere – but it will be based on what just one person has said.

Sue: And there was this occasion when I simply said on Instagram that I was going to be taking a little break from social media because the kids had just finished school for the summer – and there were these headlines saying 'Sue Radford has sensationally quit social media!' It's absolutely hilarious – and it's amazing how much they can make out of so little! There's one website that just seems to be obsessed with us. If I put a video on one of our social media accounts at night, they will have turned it into a story on their website in the morning.

Noel: They never ring us up or arrange to come round for interviews. They must have a rota of reporters who are put on 'Radford watch' – and then write 'their' stories when we post something. Reporters just seem to get so much of 'their news' from people's social media these days – without having to actually talk to the people whose quotes they are forever using. It's strange how it works.

Sue: I suppose we've just got to keep reminding ourselves that whatever we put up for our followers and subscribers will then be immediately put on a newspaper website – and then copied by other newspaper websites.

I've definitely felt tempted to abandon social media entirely. When we first started doing the TV programme and had a few negative online newspaper articles – well, it was mainly the comments underneath – I remember thinking, 'Oh, I don't want to be involved with social media, it's just such a nasty place to be.' But then you think, 'Yes, some people can be really nasty, but it's also a positive place to be because you can get so much love from it.' A lot of people really enjoy watching the show and want to pass that on. So, on the whole, I think we really like social media – but that's because we don't go looking for all the nasty stuff that we know is out there.

Noel: A while ago, we did consider taking legal action against one or two people who were hiding behind fake names and posting terrible things. Our solicitor said, 'All they will do is open another account with a different fake name, and you'll be forever chasing them.'

Sue: That all started when I was pregnant with our last child, Heidie. We shared our Christmas on Facebook and a couple of people obviously didn't like the fact we got the kids a lot of toys, while they were struggling financially. They got really nasty. They set up fake Instagram and Facebook accounts, where they were putting on really abusive stuff. Our daughter Tillie had a frame on her leg and she was really struggling to eat because she got quite depressed about her leg. One of these women commented, saying, 'It's absolutely disgusting, you want to feed your child up! She's malnourished'. You just think, 'Wow! That is really nasty.' That was quite hard to take, but it just seems that when you do well in life there are people who want to turn on you, which is really sad. But we also know we've been lucky over the years. We've got so many good friends who have really stuck with us, through good and bad times, and you know they are the people you want in your lives. They're the people who matter.

Noel: It's tricky because if you ever do answer back to the trolls, you're basically just feeding them – it's what they want. You've just got to ignore them. That's why we have this policy of 'Just keep them guessing' – when, for example, something negative has been written about us. Some people start speculating then, and want to know all the ins and outs of whatever the situation might be. But we just think the best thing to do is to say nothing. And it's quite funny to then sit back and watch as people who don't know us begin speculating and saying, 'This is going on' and, 'No, this is what is actually happening' – because they've got absolutely no idea. If you reply then they've got something else to come back at you with – because they will pick something out of your reply and have a go at you about that.

At the end of the day, yes, we are on the TV but we are entitled to a private life as well – we don't have to talk about every single thing regarding our family on the TV or on social media.

Sue: Some things are just private. But there are some more general things people have said which we're quite happy to respond to here – partly because they have really made us laugh! Here are just a few examples of the kinds of things some people say about us...

"A family of 22 kids! They must be living off the state. Imagine how much in benefits they must be getting every week."

Noel: We get zero!

Sue: If you're earning over £50,000 a year, you CAN claim child benefit – but you have to pay it all back in a child benefit tax charge, which means there is no point.

Noel: I don't even know what the child benefit rates are – I know you get so much for the first child, and less for the next – but I know it's not a big amount, so even if we weren't earning as much as we do and were eligible, it would hardly be enough to keep us in luxury! (I have just looked it up – eligible claimants will get £24 a week for their first child, and £15.90 a week for any children after that).

Sue: We haven't had child benefit for years, so it's just not relevant. It's a miniscule amount, anyway. We have had people say, 'Oh, think of all the money they must be getting' but then when they realise we own our own businesses and are doing well, they say, 'Oh, I'm really sorry, I didn't know. I just jumped to the conclusion you must be on loads of benefits.'

"They're always in Florida! They go to Florida more times than I go to the shops!"

Sue: I think it just boils down to jealousy. I have the mindset now – particularly since I lost my dad – that if you can afford to go on holiday, then go. Life is definitely too short to say, 'Oh, maybe I should squirrel my money away in the bank' or whatever. Life is too short, so just do it. If we can afford to take our kids to Florida, then we'll take our kids to Florida. I'm not going to bother myself about what other people say.

Noel: It's like you are not allowed to do things unless you have permission from the internet trolls. And it's as if people think we deserve to be kept in our place – that because we weren't born into wealth, and because we are ordinary people from an ordinary town in the North West of England, we should just be happy going to Benidorm.

"Look! They've bought a top-of-the-range motorhome – and when they're not in Florida, they're taking their kids all over the UK!"

Sue: Fancy me buying a motorhome to enable us to get away at the weekend and make special memories with our kids. How very dare we!

Noel: So, we're not allowed to go to Florida and we're not allowed to spend a weekend in the Lake District, either! I'm not sure where we're supposed to go, to be honest. Maybe we should just be staying at home and apologising for being alive!

Sue: When we bought the motorhome, so many people were like, 'You're just rubbing it in people's faces.' I'd wanted a motorhome for years and we have had to work bloody hard to be in a position where we could actually afford to buy one, so why aren't we allowed to?

"I don't know how they've managed it, but they must be millionaires!"

Noel: Some people do have an obsession about the word

'millionaire' but we just chuckle when people mention this, because we're certainly not millionaires!

"Running a pie business can't be enough to support their lifestyles!"

Sue: We are very lucky to have launched a second business. People don't realise that YouTube, Facebook, Instagram, TikTok, the Channel 5 series, brand deals and all of that, is a second income for us, we see it as our media business. The pie company is very successful, but so is the media business. As much as we love it, we don't do it just for fun, it's business at the end of the day and we are very fortunate to make a nice income from our digital content and TV series.

Noel: We've tried to get this over before – that it's not just the bakery that earns us our money. We do have other incomes, from the social media side of things and from the TV series. We would never give people figures – even ballpark figures – about what we get from the bakery, or from social media or the TV programme.

But, yes, there's the bakery, the TV show, and then we get sponsorships – they're generally from Instagram. And there will be adverts from Facebook, which is similar to what happens on YouTube.

Sue: People have said we have commercial links with Disney, but we don't do anything with Disney. We've done brand deals with Amazon and we did one with EE.

Noel: Companies will get in touch with us and if they have a product they're trying to sell, they'll give us a brief and tell us how they want us to show it off to our audience. If we genuinely like the product and think we can deliver what they're asking for then we'll agree to make some content featuring it, shoot it to their brief and we post it on our social media channels for the audience to learn more about the product.

Sue: You just film bits to do with it and talk about it on your social media. So, the more followers and the more subscribers you have the more reach you have and the more companies there are who will want to use you to get to people.

"They spoil their kids!"

Noel: We don't think we spoil them. They get their holidays, but holidays to us are precious family times. They're just times for everyone to be together. We don't gift them stuff throughout the year – they get their birthday and Christmas presents, and a packet of sweets on a Friday night! But people seem to think we're showering the kids with stuff all the time, which we don't do.

Sue: They've all been brought up to have a strong work ethic. All the older ones have gone into work after school and they're certainly not work-shy. Me and Noel have brought them up to know that they have to go out to work – if they want to buy something, then they've got to earn the money to pay for it. And the older ones who still live with us, they pay board.

All the negative comments we get on social media are usually to do with money. It seems like the second you start to do well in life, there will be people who just won't be able to accept that and they won't like it.

Noel: I remember working in my first bakery when I was 18 and someone said that all people want to know in life is how old you are and how much you earn. And my advice to people who suddenly find themselves in our position by getting a lot of media attention is to not go looking at the comments on the internet.

Sue: If you don't go looking, it's not going to hurt you, is it? But if you do go looking, then you're going to get upset.

Your message to the haters?

Noel: I'd just like them to understand we're not who they think we are.

Sue: I'd like to think if they did sit in a room with us, they would come out thinking, 'They are really lovely people and they're not who we thought they were.' Because we're not nasty people. We're just trying to do the best for our family at the end of the day. But, unfortunately, some people just don't like that very much.

I was in Sainsbury's a while ago, just minding my own business, in the cheese aisle, and this woman came up from behind me with her trolley and just looked at me and huffed, disapprovingly. I thought, 'Have I done something?' I just walked off with my trolley and then she walked past me with her trolley, turned around and gave me the most filthy, disgusted look I have ever experienced. It was like the look of someone thinking, 'I want you dead.'

I asked her, 'What's that look for?' She said, 'What look? I haven't given you a look.' I said, 'I think you have.' I went off with my trolley, and then she went around a corner and I heard her say, 'I'm sure a lot of people want to give you that look!' I just thought, 'Oh wow! I haven't done anything.' And that's the first time I've ever experienced anything like that. It really bothered me all day, and I thought, 'What have I done to deserve that?' It was awful. I just couldn't believe it. On the flipside, there was a woman I bumped into when we were camping, in nearby Silverdale, who said, 'Oh, it's Sue! It's lovely to meet you!' And things like that are just so nice. So, you get these very different people – and I know who I'd rather be.

Chapter 21

Second home dreams

Noel: We have been thinking of moving from our 10-bed house in Morecambe, which has been our home since 2004, for a good while. And it looked like there would be a major upheaval in our lives before Christmas 2023. It seemed like me and Sue would be announcing 'We HAVE moved – but, in another way, we HAVEN'T!' Yes, as ever with us, it was a bit complicated because the plan was to keep our house while buying another one a short distance away.

  Sue: We wanted to move, because we wanted more space – but we thought, 'We just can't bring ourselves to sell the house that has been our family home for so long.' The plan was to move to a new place in the countryside – heading towards Lancaster and only about a couple of miles away from the old house – in the autumn of 2023. Before we made that decision to move, we did the sums and, because we only have a relatively small mortgage on the old place, we realised we could afford to keep it. And we thought, 'If we have to sell the old house, we're not sure we would want to move at all.' It would be too hard. So many memories have been made there and so many of our children were born after we moved into it in 2004. We only had nine children when we moved in!

Noel: It was so close to happening – and we had plans for the old house long-term, involving running it as an Airbnb or renting out parts of it. But initially, the older kids who hadn't got their own places – that's Chris, Jack, Daniel and Luke – were set to continue living there, while me, Sue and the younger kids would have been in the new place. But the guy that was selling the house – his house purchase fell through and it all got a bit complicated. Also, our mortgage situation was quite complicated, and the mortgage company was getting a bit nervous – because the house we were going to buy was a lot of money.

Sue: We'll just have to wait and see what happens in the near future, because we still want to find a new place. Ideally, we will be able to keep the house we're still in now and buy a second one which, again, some of the family will move into. But if that's not possible, we may have to end up selling this house and find somewhere much bigger than the one we very nearly bought because that wasn't big enough for everyone currently living here. But I really do hope we can keep this place. My special memories are all to do with watching the kids growing up here – all the family Christmases and the kids' birthdays. All the occasions we have celebrated together, and watched the kids come down those stairs on Christmas morning.

Noel: I remember, when we moved in, Millie, who was about to celebrate her third birthday, could walk underneath the worktop in the kitchen – and obviously she's a fully-grown adult now. Then, in later years, you'd see the other ones, when they were only small, being able to walk underneath it. It always took us back – and made us think of Millie and how young and how small she was when we moved in.

Sue: The house is obviously known as the house people see on *Britain's Biggest Family: 22 Kids and Counting*, and we have had so many people drive past, take pictures and film videos. We have even had people turning up at the house to say 'Hi.'

Noel: And as the viewers have seen, we have put a lot of work into the house to make it an even better place to live. We're proud of the garden, because it was awful when we moved in. All around the back it was just concrete and the front was just a muddy grass patch. There was nowhere for the kids to play. And it wasn't safe for the kids, either – there was no gate on the drive and it was quite insecure. We're also proud of the improvements we have made to the kitchen. That was also bloody awful when we moved in.

Sue: The dining room used to be a bedroom with an en suite and we totally transformed that. When we think about it, we really have done an awful lot to this house – including refurbishing all the bedrooms.

Noel: We turned the outside of the house into a real entertainment complex – with the pool and the bar – and it's a place the kids love to play. But of course it has its downsides – the maintenance is never-ending! It's a bit like the Forth Bridge – you are just constantly going round repainting and redecorating. Then there's having to feed the electricity meter, and being plunged into darkness on a regular basis!

Sue: So many people have watched the house tour videos we put on YouTube. But people are like me, I think – they're nosey! I love looking at other people's houses on the internet and I love TV programmes which feature people's houses. It's just curiosity – and it also gives you good ideas. And people do get in touch all the time, asking things like, 'Where do you get your dining tables from?', 'Where are your chairs from?' and things like that.

Noel: If we do ever have to sell the house, I think it would be a weird feeling driving past it after moving out. We'd be thinking about all the memories it gave us, and we'd be wondering about how things were going for the new owners.

Sue: I remember when we bought it, Noel's mum walked in and said, 'You can tell as soon as you walk in it's such a warm family home' – and that's what we always feel about it.

Noel: I think if we do ever sell it, it won't be kept as one house – I'm sure it would be split into four flats.

Sue: The kitchen is my favourite room. You might be watching telly with the kids, or just chatting away with them while you're cooking – it's a place where everyone likes to gather.

Noel: Everyone loves being in the kitchen, sitting together and having a good laugh.

Sue: I remember when we first moved in, someone said to us, 'Ooh, you'll have to fill all these bedrooms!' And I said, 'We will do – don't worry about that!' The place we nearly moved to is so different. It's a 16th century house, with all these wooden beams. It's got so much character. It's really lovely.

Noel: It isn't far from a residential area, but I'd describe it as being in the open countryside. It does have two neighbouring houses, and we would have been glad about that if we had moved there. Some people might think – because we had said we wanted a house with nothing around it – that the only downside to that place would have been that it has neighbouring properties. But we thought having that bit of security – with some people close by rather than us being in complete isolation – would have been a positive, really.

Our house search has always been about trying to find more space, and in a more rural and open area – we found one place that was great because it had about seven acres of land, but it backed onto the motorway and the traffic was obviously constant. Another one had three or four acres but it was on the wrong side of Lancaster. It would have been nice having so much extra space outdoors if the move had gone ahead – I remember when we first saw the place we were going to buy, the kids were just running around outside. I think the garden area was about one acre in total.

Sue: There was a lot more outdoor space, and lots more parking. The driveway kind of wrapped around the house. We said, when we first stood outside it, that we couldn't believe that we could be buying a place like this. It felt quite surreal to be there. We even got as far as telling Channel 5 they had to be really careful about how they filmed it, so people couldn't tell exactly where 'our new house' was. There were six bedrooms, but we had been planning to turn it into a nine-bed house.

Noel: There would have been 14 kids living in that house, compared to the 18 we have here – as Sophie, Chloe and Millie have left.

Sue: I think everyone would have been happy. The kids who were going to move with us would have loved all the extra room – especially outside – while the older kids would have loved having this place to themselves.

Noel: And because we would have only been up the road, the older ones would always have been popping round – so there wouldn't have been that much change at all, really. We were just looking forward to a change of lifestyle. Because of the lack of space here, the kids are often just inside on their computers – but the place we nearly bought presented more opportunities for them to be outside.

At first, we were looking to build somewhere but that was never going to happen because the plots of land were so expensive – or, if you found one, it was snapped up straight away by an investor. And the cost of building materials has just shot up in recent years.

Sue: We did even mention the idea of moving to Florida on the programme. It was definitely more than a pipe dream to buy somewhere there and I would definitely still like to live there one day. But I think buying a house in this country is the main priority for now.

Noel: This is the place we know. I do like Florida, but I'm probably a bit less enthusiastic than Sue about buying something there. I think if we're going to buy somewhere in the sun I'd prefer to buy somewhere in Europe – somewhere that's a bit cheaper and easier to get to. Somewhere where you could just hop on a plane and go for a long weekend. But we know that, if we do end up with a second home, some people online won't be happy with us!

It's like, if you have worked your way up to be able to do something like that, you're somehow not allowed it. But if you're one of these people on the TV who have always had money, then it's fine – it's expected of them. For some reason, we're not allowed to spend the money we've earned – or to enjoy it. We shouldn't be able to buy cars, houses or go on holiday, apparently.

Sue: People say about us, 'They've changed, they're not the same anymore' – but we are! It's just that we now have the means to buy things and to go to places.

Noel: And what, really, is wrong with that?

Chapter 22

A day in the life
of Sue and Noel

Sue: At first, we were going to write this as two separate chapters
– *A day in the life of Sue* and *A day in the life of Noel*.

But we quickly came to realise it would make far more sense
to write it as a joint chapter, because for so much of our time
we work as a double act – even if we can be so busy that we can
sometimes barely get the chance to have a proper conversation
with each other from one day to the next.

Noel: I've got the pie business to go out and spend time at
each day – a bakehouse and a shop, although I mostly spend
my time in the bakehouse – but because I'm my own boss, I'm
able to be at home at two crucial times of the day. These are the
Radfords' morning rush hour and the Radfords' afternoon rush
hour!

Sue: Noel is always there to help me get the kids off to school
every morning – and always there to help me get them all

home again, and he's here to stay once they are home in the afternoon.

Noel: We are lucky. If I wasn't self-employed, it just wouldn't work. Can you imagine me, working for a company – I don't think I'd be able to say to the boss, 'Listen, if it's OK with you I'll need to be available to do the school runs twice a day – don't worry, I'll fit them around my duties in the workplace somehow.'

Sue: It just wouldn't happen, would it? Having our own business is part of what makes everything work for us – and we realise how fortunate we are, because we know there are a lot of other families with real childcare issues because one or both parents need to be in work at around the times their children are going to, or coming home from, nursery and school.

5.30am-5.40am

Noel: This is when I usually wake up – though that isn't the plan. I do have an alarm clock but, annoyingly, I always wake up before it goes off. The alarm will normally be set for 6am, or maybe 6.10am. I might try to have a snooze, but I sometimes just get up straight away. I don't bother with breakfast, and I won't even have a cup of coffee. I will usually quickly check my emails in case things have come through during the night that need to be sorted out – details regarding deliveries and things like that.

6.30am-6.45am

Noel: I tend to arrive at work – about a 15-minute drive away – about this time. Apart from those times when one or two of the kids were leaving at the same time as me to come to the bakery,

I've always been up and out before anybody else in the house is awake – so it's never felt strange that the house is quiet. It's that moment of the day when, if I was to have a cup of coffee, it would be great – such a lovely and peaceful time to do it. The problem is, I can't face coffee at that time of the day, so you could say I don't really make the most of it! Once I'm at the bakehouse, I'll work out what we need to do that day – and then I'll do a quick cash and carry run on the way back home for the morning rush hour chaos with the kids!.

7am-8.30am

Noel: Thankfully, I'll be at work when the chaos at home begins! But by around 7.50am-8am, I'm back home again to help Sue with the kids – making sure they have their breakfasts and get washed, dressed and ready for school. It's a very different scene to the peaceful one I left about 90 minutes earlier. It's carnage! Some mornings are better than others, but it's the worst time of the day in my opinion, because you're really up against the clock.

Sue: It makes his time at work look tame by comparison! But there's some real teamwork when Noel arrives back, because he'll help get some of the kids ready so we don't end up with anyone being late for school.

Noel: Sue's there trying to get everyone up and fed, and we're still having to drag a few out of bed as well. It can, depending on the day, be relatively quiet – or it can be hell. If our youngest, Heidie, in particular, has got out of bed on the wrong side and is in a foul mood as a result, we can be in real trouble.

Sue: I normally get up about 7am – get myself ready and put a bit of make-up on, and then start getting the kids out of bed.

Some of them are definitely easier than others. Usually, Oscar is one of the worst to get out of bed – Hallie is another one who likes her bed. But the rest of them, thankfully, are not too bad. Max and Tillie, for example, are normally organised and getting themselves ready. Then it's a question of getting everyone downstairs and sorting their breakfasts out. The older ones will have taken all of the bowls and spoons to their bedrooms, so then you're searching around the house trying to find bowls and spoons so everyone else can have their breakfast. I'll go and get the ones that have been left in the older boys' bedrooms and will have to wash them – while some of the kids are waiting for their breakfasts. And they all like different things, so it's just absolute chaos.

Noel: You'll say to one of them, 'What do you want for breakfast?' and they'll just stare at you. Maybe they're still half asleep. And you go, 'Right, I'll have to come back to you in a minute.'

Sue: Some will want porridge, some will want Chocolate Rice Krispies, some will want Weetabix, some will want toast. It's absolutely crazy. Luckily no one ever takes the mickey by asking for a Full English – if they did, they'd be on their bikes! We do have them doing things in a particular order; they'll have their breakfasts first, then the older ones can be left to go upstairs to get themselves dressed and ready while I will help the smaller ones get ready. And the kids will also have to make their beds and tidy their bedrooms and then wash themselves and brush their teeth. Then they come back downstairs – and they then TRY to find their shoes and coats, which isn't as easy as some people might think. There always seems to be shoes missing, and shoes are often seen flying everywhere as the kids try to find theirs. It's always bedlam by the shoe racks. After breakfast,

I'll be tidying the breakfast things away and sorting the kids' lunchboxes, water bottles and the bags they take to school. Then I'll have to sort their hair out – that can take a good 10 minutes.

Noel: And it's always been the same amount of chaos over the years – there haven't really been quieter spells – because we've always had several kids in primary school at the same time.

Sue: Yeah, it's always been like this for about as long as we can remember! But while, like Noel, I won't have any breakfast, we do somehow find the time to grab a cup of coffee about 8am, just after he's arrived back from work to help me out with the kids.

8.15am-9am

Noel: This is where it gets tricky trying to explain, because we can have various arrangements in play regarding minding some of the grandkids. We currently have three grandkids staying the night with us, and I'll take them to school around this time. It varies with the grandkids – at the moment, Daisy, Ayprill and Leo, who are Sophie's kids, are staying over with us because their mum and dad are doing early morning work shifts. But normally my mornings would be me going to work, but then picking those three up from their mum and dad's about 7am, and then doing my cash and carry run later. But whoever I'm taking, I have to be gone by 8.15am. But we always seem to be late – every single day. Like Sue says, there is a routine – the breakfasts, getting dressed and washing and getting their hair done – but in between, there is always a battle to keep them from playing on their tablets. You think they're ready but you'll see one who has no shoes and socks on and he's staring at a screen. I hate being late, especially getting the kids to school –

not least because it also puts me behind my schedule for work. Of course, it's much easier for me during the school holidays because, then, I don't need to take that break in my working day and get home by 8am. That's much easier.

Sue: It's always around 8.45am that things get especially stressful. I am trying to leave the house by this time, having made sure the kids have all got their shoes on and have everything ready. I then take our younger kids to their school – Oscar, Casper, Hallie, Phoebe, Archie and Bonnie are all in school and Heidie is in nursery. I know if they are not out of the house by this time then we are going to be late – and the school gate shuts at five-to-nine. Then you've got to go to the reception to sign in. So, I HAVE to be out of the house by quarter-to. We always manage to do it somehow, but it is so stressful – and I am just repeatedly shouting, 'Get your shoes on! Get your water bottle! Get your bag!'

Noel: The worst mornings are when, just before they're supposed to be leaving the house, one of the kids will say, 'I can't find one of my shoes' and you look and see that his or her brother or sister has got two left shoes on!

Sue: I think I've only ever been late once, and that was when we couldn't find a pair of Oscar's shoes and I ended up having to put his trainers on him – and we never did find those shoes, did we, Noel?

Noel: No, they STILL haven't turned up!

9am–3pm (Noel)

Noel: By now, I'll be back in work mode. The first thing I'll do is go to the shop, taking stuff from the cash and carry. Then it's the short drive back to the bakehouse and the rest of the working day is just making pies – and that's it, really. My working life is certainly easier than my home life – especially helping to sort the kids at breakfast. I'd probably prefer to do 12 hours at the bakehouse than do breakfast time at home! But no, seriously, I do quite enjoy it. There are days when you think you might explode because of one thing or another, but no – things usually go pretty smoothly. At lunchtime, someone might take pity on me and make me a sandwich, and I'll get another cup of coffee. But I just tend to work through, really.

9am-noon (Sue)

Sue: I'm back home about now – but sadly not to watch any daytime telly, or to have a long lie down in a dark room! The first thing I'll do is tidy up the shoe rack because there will be shoes everywhere, then I'll start tidying up in the kitchen, dining room and living room. I'll set the dishwasher off, start Hoovering, mop the floors and generally tidy up. Then I'll move onto the first lot of bedrooms, the boys' rooms. I'll get all of the washing from them, Hoover and tidy, clean the bathroom and take pots down that the kids have left in their rooms. Then I'll go to the girls' rooms, which are always a nightmare – a right mess. That will all take me forever to sort out, then I'll clean the bathroom by these bedrooms. I'll then Hoover up there, and then go and put all the dirty washing in the two big washing machines and set them off. I'll then take the dry washing out of the tumble dryer, fold it all and put it away. That just carries on throughout the day. The thing about the washing is that I've got to do it all together, rather than getting all the kids involved. Because if, say, one of the kids wanted to look after themselves and do their washing separately then that would take up a washing machine. So, it makes more sense to do it all together – which means me doing it. But some of the older ones are good at helping me out – Ellie, for example, is good at helping me put washing away.

Also, whereas I'm sure there must be couples who are able to ring each other up during the day to discuss various things about their kids, Noel and I really don't speak when he's at work and I'm at home – because we never have the time. And sometimes we don't even have the time to speak to each other when we're both at home!

Noon-3pm (Sue)

Sue: I'll usually finish the general housework, and then have a bit of dinner while waiting for the washing machines to finish so I can put the washing in the tumble dryer. I'll sit down for about half an hour and then I'll sort the laundry out. And there's always mountains of stuff to put away every single day. There must be at least five piles of washing done every day.

3pm-6pm

Noel: I'll get home in time to help Sue with the afternoon school run. And actually, if we are able to be in the minibus together, this is probably one of the only times we are guaranteed to get to talk to each other during the day – on our way to school, literally for around five or 10 minutes! You can't do it on the way back because all the kids are telling us about their days.

Sue: It's a great help having Noel back for the school run – and again, we know that we wouldn't be able to do this if Noel was working for an ordinary company in an ordinary nine to five job. There are some things that Noel has had to miss because he's been busy at work – like end of year assemblies where the kids have won prizes – but having another pair of hands there for the two school runs is priceless.

Overall, my day does tend to go smoothly, but there are days when the time seems to run away from you and you're left thinking, 'I've just got so much still to do.' That can be the case when we're doing a lot of filming for the TV series.

Noel: Once you get the kids home, it's like breakfast time all over again – just chaos! I'm at home for good now, I don't go back to work. But, to be honest, it's not too bad.

Sue: It's just a case, before the evening meal, of keeping the kids from raiding the fridge, freezer and food cupboards.

Noel: There'll be kids wanting to help themselves to a bowl of cereal, grab a biscuit, make a sandwich or whatever. It seems like this is the time of day when kids feel really hungry – between coming home and having their evening meal. But they're not too bad, and a lot of them will just quietly go off to their rooms because they want to play on their tablets or whatever – while others might go and play outside.

6pm-11pm

Sue: We like to be sat down for our tea by 6pm, with everyone finished at 6.30pm, because bath time for the younger ones is 6.45pm.

Noel: And we just make the one meal – it's not a hotel where people can have whatever they want. We will discuss what people fancy that evening, and people will give their suggestions. It's just a case of making what you think will get eaten most. Some of the go-to meals that will get us through the week will be a spaggy bol because that goes down well with everybody, a pesto chicken dish with noodles, a potato bake that I make, and jacket potatoes. The kids love all of those. We very rarely have a proper pudding – maybe yoghurts and things like that. We just find if you do puddings, it's much more washing up!

Sue: Luckily, the kids are not fussy eaters – they like all kinds of food, really.

Noel: But some of the older ones will often make their own tea now – they don't want to be associated with us anymore!

Sue: Yes, once the kids get to about 17 or 18 – that's when they want to look after themselves at meal times.

Noel: But we've found that's usually more the boys than the girls.

Sue: For bath time, these days, it's probably seven of them I'll need to do. Then, when they've had their baths and got their pyjamas on, they'll want their supper! By now it will be about half-seven, and they'll be wanting something like a bowl of cereal before they go to bed. Hallie, Phoebe, Archie, Bonnie and Heidie will all go to bed soon after half-seven, and the rest of the younger kids will go about half-eight or nine. The teenagers will obviously go a lot later than that.

Noel: We'll sit with the little ones until they've gone to sleep. We try to aim for about half-eight for the little ones to have all gone off to sleep, although it can get to after nine. But then there's always something else to do – usually the garden to tidy up, because there will be bikes and scooters left out. And there are other things you might need to sort out – emails, for example. If everything has gone OK with the youngest kids at bedtime, then me and Sue would like to be able to sit down and have a cup of tea together as soon after half-eight as we can. Sometimes that's the case, sometimes it isn't.

Sue: We've also got to make sure all their uniforms are out and ready for the morning – and after the little ones have had their baths there will then be more of their stuff for me to put in the wash.

Noel: Our own bedtime is probably between 10 and 11. We can often say at 10, 'Shall we go to bed?' but will end up watching something else on the telly for another half hour. Or we might make the effort to make another cup of tea and then take it up and watch another episode of one of our favourite shows in bed – *Benidorm*. We love that show! But there can be nights when we've not really had any time to ourselves away from the chores.

It all depends how chaotic the day has been and what the little ones have been like at bedtime. But Friday evenings and nights are a lot more relaxed – the routine isn't the same, and the timings aren't the same as they are during the school week.

Sue: And we love the weekends, when we can all do things together.

Noel: If the weather is nice, it's brilliant because it means you can get out and about. But if it's miserable and wet, it's hard work and you feel sorry for the kids. I remember myself when I was a kid – when it rained I was bored. Of course, our lot have got each other to play with but it's not the same.

Sue: As for when we get the food shopping in – we don't have a set day for the big shop. We go to the shops pretty much every day for the essentials – things like bread, milk and fruit. I used to do the big shop all online – an Asda delivery – but it got so expensive, so I go to Aldi now. But because I can't get everything that I used to get in one go online from Asda, I have to go a few times during the week. But it still works out cheaper to do that, though it is time-consuming compared to the convenience of doing it online.

Noel: I think one of our top-ups is probably like another family's weekly shopping!

Sue: Also, our days can be very different if we're in the middle of filming – because the crew can be here from about 1pm through to about 7pm or 8pm. Some days it can be quite difficult, because the kids will have different things on and you've got to sort tea out or go and get a bit of shopping. And that can have a knock-on effect because we might have to delay tea or bath-time.

Noel: Our YouTube videos tend to be done at weekends, unless it's something like a simple question and answer session which me and Sue might sit down and do at 8.30pm. Otherwise, it's the weekends pretty much.

Sue: We normally won't have a bath until we can relax, after 8.30pm – because the older girls won't have theirs normally until after the kids' bath-time.

Noel: You do get to the end of the night sometimes and just think, 'We've not stopped all day, from the second we got up.' And then it's a case of, 'Let's do it all again tomorrow!' I think we both need a lie down, Sue, after going through a typical day in our lives – but sadly, we haven't got time.

Chapter 23

How much?!? Christmas, birthdays and buying Porsches

Noel: As I think we have established, people can be very interested in how much things cost – and we're no different.

Things can obviously get very expensive in our family – not least when birthdays come around, and at Christmas. People might assume it's especially a nightmare for our poor kids – having to buy presents for so many siblings. But sensibly, I think, none of our kids buy their brothers and sisters anything on their birthdays.

At Christmas time, though, Sophie, Chloe, Luke and Millie have always been the older ones who will get every sibling something. But the other older ones? Nah, it's too much effort! I know it can be expensive and they don't need to do it, but those four have always just wanted to do it. We've always left it to them.

Sue: But at Christmas, even some of the younger ones will be given a little bit of money to buy something small for their siblings. Though our kids don't tend to buy their nieces and nephews anything on their birthdays or at Christmas, we will buy presents for the grandkids.

Noel: And I suppose we have a rough budget worked out in our heads for when we buy presents for our kids. For birthdays, it's probably around £100 to £150 for every child – something like that. It might be a bit more or a bit less. It depends on what they want. For example, for Phoebe's last birthday, she picked out some things that were cheap and cheerful.

Sue: Yeah, she wanted craft-type things to play with – and a pair of roller boots – but hers were not as expensive as what some of the other kids have wanted. It just depends on what they want, really, but we try not to go over £150 for any of them. And we will often have either a party or an outing on someone's birthday – it just depends on what they want to do.

Noel: Some of them may want to go to the trampoline park, or a place like that – but we don't generally have parties at home with other kids coming round, because we've got enough of our own to make a birthday party! I think, as they get older, it's probably more the boys who begin to want less of a fuss on their birthdays. The girls will usually want either a party or to go out somewhere.

Sue: It's like Josh – he just said he'd prefer to go shopping with his mates. When they get to a certain age, they're not really bothered about birthday parties. Then, regarding presents, when the kids get to about 19 or 20, they'll normally just get some money from us.

Noel: And to be fair, the kids do spoil us on our birthdays. They always make sure they get us something, even if it's just a small box of chocolates or something.

Sue: They always make the effort to get us something, and we think that's really nice. And you'll often come down to balloons in the living room and flowers and chocolates. They're really thoughtful.

Noel: We wouldn't tend to have a party to mark my birthday, because it's on Christmas Eve and we're all getting geared up for Christmas Day.

Sue: For mine, we'll just ask the kids if they want something special for tea and then all have a nice meal together. October is the big birthday month in the house, because four of the kids have birthdays in October. It's a very busy and expensive time – and you really don't need that expense when you're starting to think about Christmas! To be honest, I'm really glad when that month is over – because that's when I'll normally be able to start concentrating on doing the bulk of the Christmas shopping. But I will have actually started getting bits and pieces in for Christmas in September and October – but it's when the birthdays are over in October that I'll start turning my mind to the bigger presents.

Noel: Sue will do all the present shopping – everything. But I will join her in shopping for the food we'll need over Christmas. We don't really budget for it – we don't have a set amount. We dread to think how much it's all going to add up to, but it's Christmas so you do want to throw the once-a-year treats in the trolley without thinking too much about what it's all going to cost.

Sue: And with the presents, the kids always have to write their Christmas lists nice and early – so Santa has an idea what he's going to be up against. But then again, if we ask them to do this too early, you'll generally find that they change their minds and it'll be, 'Oh, I don't really want that anymore,' so that can be a bit awkward. But the lists will tend to be put together in October.

Noel: It used to be easier years ago – remember when we got the Argos catalogue, and they would cut things out of it and stick them on a piece of paper for us? Now, they write things down – then replace them the next day with a whole new list. There comes a point when Sue has to say, 'Right, that's it, you can't change your list anymore. Santa needs to know now!'

Sue: Like with the food, we don't have a definite budget in mind for the presents. And, to be honest, for the last few years we have cut back a little bit on the presents, because we've gone to Disneyland Paris in the build-up to Christmas – about a week or so before. And we've been to Lapland before, around that time. Those trips represent the kids' big Christmas treat. Then, on Christmas Day, they'll just have one main present and some smaller ones – and we think that's much better for the kids, and for us.

We don't end up spending as much, but I'll probably still end up getting through about 70 rolls of Christmas wrapping paper – and I hate wrapping presents! The kids love those trips – and they also love going shopping for the Christmas food. But the thing is, you can't take them all because it would be chaos – all the kids would be chucking everything in the trolley. So, we generally just take a few of them with us now, which makes it all a bit easier.

Noel: I'll usually get the turkey from my butcher, but pretty much everything else we'll get when we go out to do the big Christmas shop together. I always say the Christmas dinner is just a Sunday roast with parsnips and sprouts. So, once we've got all that and a couple of puddings, we're sorted. People wonder how big our dinner is – well, I'll get a turkey crown of about six kilos (around 13 pounds), along with a gammon of about three and a half kilos (nearly eight pounds) and a piece of beef, which will be a similar size.

Sue: We'll decorate the house downstairs with three Christmas trees – and there will be trees in three or four of the kids' bedrooms, as well. And on the trees, there will be personalised baubles in memory of Alfie and my dad and Noel's mum.

Noel: Everyone will be together on Christmas Day – including all the kids and grandkids, pretty much – and it is crazy, but in a great way. There must be around 40 of us in the house.

Sue: Things have to be pretty well-organised on Christmas morning because of how many kids there are in the house – so, they will have put their pillow cases out the night before, and they'll leave carrots for the reindeer and a drink for Santa. Then, they'll go to bed. Me and Noel will come downstairs first thing in the morning and we'll wait at the door of the living room. Then we all pile in together at the same time, once all the kids are together and ready to see what Santa has brought them. It's just wonderful, and we really can't explain how much we love it!

Noel: You just can't beat Christmas in our house – and we get just as excited as the kids. They did get up as early as 5.30am in years gone by, but we were like, 'No, you'll have to go back to bed – Santa might not have been yet.' Now it's about 7.30am – which, we know, some families might think is pretty late, thinking about their own kids. But that seems to be the kind of time that our kids have settled on as their Christmas morning routine. Actually, it has been as late as 8am on some occasions. Though sometimes, you can hear one or two of them outside the bedroom door – 'No, you go and wake mum and dad!'

Sue: Most of the older ones like to get up early, too.

Noel: And the kids who have left home will tend to be with us around noon. There isn't a set time for getting round the table, but we generally aim for about 3pm. Lunch is just ready when it's ready, because there's so much going on you can't plan things too precisely. We'll find ourselves playing with the kids' toys – or we're just chatting in the kitchen, and the kids are off doing their own thing. I don't do the dinner on my own – Sue will be helping, and some of the girls like to help, too.

Sue: The kids will all be playing with their own toys for most of the day and it will be different things for different age groups – but usually, at night time, there'll be a chance to get the Monopoly or another board game out and we'll play that with the older kids.

Noel: Or it might be a Scalextric – just something a few of us can play together. But because there's so much going on in the house, the younger kids are frightened of missing out on something so they will be trying to stay awake and stay up for as long as they possibly can. And there's no chance of mum and dad grabbing a few minutes for a little snooze. The action is just non-stop – it'll be, 'Mum, can you do this?' and, 'Dad, have you got batteries for this – how does this work?' But we don't mind, because we just love Christmas.

Sue: It's so special all being together, and for me and Noel to see all the kids so happy and excited – it must be the best day of the year. I always remember Christmas at my house, with my late dad always being asleep on a chair with his mouth open! And that was after getting up late, because he never liked to be up early with me and my brother.

Noel: I don't think your dad and Christmas got on, did they?

Sue: But, no, when he came round to ours for Christmas before he passed away, he did love it. He loved the chaos of it all.

Noel: I think the older he got, the more he enjoyed it.

Sue: Christmas has always been special for our family. I know a lot of people make a big deal about New Year's Eve, but we never have.

Noel: It's nothing like Christmas, is it? Some years, everyone will come round and we'll have a bit of a do, or watch the fireworks at midnight. But other years, we can just be sitting here, quite chilled.

Sue: Or we'll all just have an early night. And then, this all leads into 'no-spend January' – and none of the kids have birthdays in January or February, which really helps. I quite like to do a no-spend January, because I think after the expense of all those birthdays in October and then Christmas, it's just so nice to have a quiet month. I think it's good for the kids, too, as they grow up. We've always brought them up to appreciate the value of hard work and getting jobs. And I think it's also good that they see that while you can have some indulgence on your birthday and at Christmas, you have to have times in the year when you're not spending and when you're saving up instead to pay for things you want at the special times of the year.

Noel: It's difficult for us to have precise budgets. For the big weekly shop, we'll just have to get in what we need. But it's the daily top-ups where we have to be more careful. And regarding the treats, we will tell the kids, 'Once they're gone, they're gone. We won't be buying any more until next week.' I think the big shop, now, is getting up to about £300.

Sue: I think it's more than that. With the top-ups, in total, it's probably around £450 a week – though that's at the time of writing, and things can go up very quickly. When I used to do a big online shop with Asda, I'd notice it could suddenly be an extra £40 a week. It was crazy.

Noel: And we'll go to the little Asda for the daily top-ups we need – the bread, milk and fruit. We can actually get through between 12 and 18 pints of milk every day – it's a good job we have a double-fridge!

Sue: And during the school holidays, however much we think we have topped it up, you can come down in the morning and find there's only a drop of milk left in the house. The kids get through so much of it. Maybe we get through more than that amount.

Noel: But we probably don't buy as many potatoes as people think – I'll do bakes with potatoes in them, but we're not massive fans of potato dishes, really. I'd say, we get about 15 or 20 kilos a week – 20 kilos is about 44 pounds. So, yeah, that might sound a lot to some families! We are also often asked about how we get around – what transport we use to ferry ourselves and the kids around. It's a bit of a mixture, really – it's not just about purely functional vehicles, because I've had a passion for cars from being a child.

We did have a Land Rover – that was a 46th birthday present for Sue – but we got rid of that, and bought a Porsche to replace it. Then we got rid of the Porsche, and we replaced it with another one. Then we got rid of that Porsche, because it was crap. Then, a bit later, in September 2023, we got another Porsche!

From being very young, I always loved the idea of one day being able to have a Porsche. But on the more functional, everyday front, we still have the minibus and the motorhome.

Sue: And what colour is the latest Porsche, Noel?

Noel: It's pink! Well, officially, they call it 'frozen berry'! It's certainly turning a few heads in Morecambe.

Sue: People do love it. We went to a campsite soon after we got it, and this couple tracked us down after walking all around the campsite - because they had seen Noel driving it in and wanted to tell us how much they loved the colour!

Noel: A lot of people do love the colour. I don't take it to work very often, but I remember doing so a couple of months after we got it - and this delivery guy, who was built like a brick shithouse, told me 'Wow! I love the colour of that car!' It's an electric one – a Taycan Turismo. We had been thinking of getting a Discovery, because they are more practical, but we think 'Discos' are too expensive to run.

The first Porsche we had was a Porsche Cayenne Coupe, which is a hybrid. It was really nice, but we just fancied changing it. We'd had it for 12 months. We swapped it for a Porsche Taycan Turbo – that's all electric and we just had a few problems with it, so it went back. We had it for two months, but it was in the garage for four weeks of that time. They call it a Turbo, but there's no Turbo because it's electric.

And the ones we've bought have been five-seaters - so they are quite practical as well.

I always wanted a Porsche from being a kid, when I had a picture of a Porsche 911 on my bedroom wall. I said to my mum one day, 'I want to get a Porsche.' And I ended up getting one – but it wasn't a 911!

Sue: When we picked that first brand new Porsche up out of the garage – and we'd had to wait about seven months for it to be ready – we looked at each other and both said 'Wow!' We never ever thought we would end up owning something like that. It was crazy.

Noel: The garage is on the way to Kendal and we'd be going through to see Sue's mum or my dad, and we'd drive past it and often say, 'I don't think we'll ever be able to go in there!'

The minibus is great for us, because we can get nine in it. The motorhome – you can drive with six people in it, but we've had about 12 to 14 sleeping in it.

Sue: Yes, but because it can just take six for driving, I'll be driving behind with some other kids.

Noel: The thing is, we're still in love with Porsche cars. The first one we had was a metallic grey and the second a metallic dark blue. But Sue loved the look of the pink one they had.

Sue: You were like, 'I don't really know if I like this colour.'

Noel: I know, but I do now – and it certainly stands out!

Chapter 24

"Is it a school trip?" Out and about with the kids

Noel: They say you can get used to anything in life – but I'm not sure 'anything' includes getting from A to B with an army of kids in tow! To some extent, we have learned to roll with it, but that doesn't mean it has got any easier over the years. After so many testing experiences, we just know what to expect now – and are ready to grit our teeth and brace ourselves in a bid to get through the pain and hassle.

I think being at airports and travelling on trains are our least favourite experiences when we have lots of the kids with us. Airports are bad purely because of when you queue up to hand in your passports and to check-in – it's really stressful and hard work. Once that's done, we're fine – probably like a lot of people. But the stress of this part of going away is probably multiplied for us, because of the numbers of people involved. There is far more admin, basically – and no one likes admin! But seriously, it can be horrendous.

Sue: As Noel mentioned in an earlier chapter, we've had problems at the check-in desk when presenting a big pile of passports. They do sometimes look at you like they're thinking, 'What on earth is going on here?' On that occasion Noel was referring to, when he was explaining he didn't like rude people, the guy behind the desk said one half of us would have to go and join a different queue and check-in at that desk.

Noel: It's just us arriving as one big group that they don't seem to like. But splitting us up just creates other problems, not least for the check-in staff. There may have been a lot of us but what seemed to have been forgotten on that occasion was that we were all on one booking. The guy behind the desk who asked us to split up into two queues was logging in on his computer trying to check half of us in, and the woman at the other desk was doing the same for the other half. But it took about an hour to sort this out, simply because a family under one booking was being dealt with by two different people.

Sue: The second group of us ended up having to go back to the original check-in desk, so the man who had caused the delay ended up having to check us all in together anyway.

Noel: It really was pathetic.

Sue: We also had a really bad experience on a train to London once. We ended up having to stand – with all the kids – because there were no seats available.

Noel: Yes, it's not so much the train stations that cause us problems – it's the trains themselves because they are often so busy, and because there will be so many of us. We were invited to appear on ITV's *This Morning* programme, and they got our train tickets from Lancaster to London sorted out for us. The only stops before we got on were Edinburgh, Carlisle and Oxenholme, but the train was absolutely rammed. There were at least 18 to 20 in our party – some of us were standing by the toilets, while some were in between the carriages where the floor wobbles. And that was it for the whole journey.

Sue: It was a nightmare. In fact, we very nearly got off at Preston – the next stop – because I thought it wasn't safe for the kids. That was really bad – a terrible experience, and very stressful when you have so many children with you all standing up for that length of time.

Noel: Regarding people's attitudes when they come across me, Sue and a load of kids out in public, I'd say when we do experience problems it tends to be a mix – involving people who find it stressful serving us and dealing with us, and then other members of the public who are at the same places we've gone to.

We do tend to feel embarrassed when we're all queuing up for something as we're conscious the people behind us are going to have to wait longer than they might normally have to. But then we try to tell ourselves, 'Well, if we were three different families in front of them, they would still have to wait the same amount of time.' It does bother you, but then we think, 'This is how it is. We're a big family – we can't help it.'

Sue: It's obviously been like this for a number of years now, but you're still really conscious of other people in situations like this – if you're going for ice creams for the kids or something, and you're creating a big queue. You're thinking, 'Oh God, all these people behind us are going to be really annoyed.' But because of the number of times this has happened, you do develop a thick skin. You just have to get on with it, and hope you're not creating too much of a problem for anybody else.

Noel: Yeah, you've just got to put your blinkers on and look straight ahead – don't try to catch the eyes of the people who might be glaring at you! Cinemas are a typical place where there can be queueing issues – while, as other families will know, there is also the issue of all the food and drink being pretty expensive! I know much smaller families take in their own sweets, but it's a bit of a mix with us because it can often be a last-minute decision for us to go to the cinema. So, sometimes, we may end up having to fork out for a lot of stuff when we're there. Otherwise, it might be a case of someone running round to the little Asda nearby and getting all the packets of sweets.

Sue: We might just get some popcorn and a drink when we're in there. But it's also quite funny at the cinema because we can obviously take up whole rows of seats.

Noel: I remember when we went to watch *Barbie* a while back – there were no queues when we got there but by the time we'd been served with some sweets, there was a big queue behind us and we're thinking 'Oh God!' again.

But when we're out and about on holiday and looking for somewhere to eat, we've pretty much learned where we can and can't go. We always look to try to find somewhere to sit outside – like pub beer gardens – or a place which we know is going to be big and family-friendly, like a Toby Carvery. In those sorts of places, they're used to kids coming in – although they may not be used to so many coming in as part of the same family! Pizza Express is another place that caters for families well, so we've been to their restaurants, too. We wouldn't just rock up at a nice, intimate restaurant somewhere that wasn't designed for big families.

Sue: The big thing we've always got to be conscious of is finding somewhere that's going to have the number of tables we'll need to seat us all. In Florida, we found there were places where you could only book for eight people at a time so we had to do a number of bookings. It can all get a bit complicated, depending where you are and what rules they have in place for how many people they can cater for in one group. Ideally, you want one big long table where we can all sit together at the same time.

Noel: Different restaurants have different set-ups regarding booking – and whether you can book. If we're in a Disney-themed resort in Florida, you have to pre-book the restaurants. But at other places, where there may be no booking involved, it will be a case of one of us putting our heads in and asking if they can take 20 people, or however many of us there are. Often, because we do try to go to big, family-friendly places, it can just be a matter of waiting 10 minutes or so.

Sue: Obviously there will be occasions in this country – like if we're in the Lake District, perhaps – where there isn't a big place like a Toby Carvery or a Pizza Express where we can go with all the kids, so we won't go to restaurants in those situations.

Noel: We'll just have a picnic somewhere, because that will be the easiest thing to do. We have had people joking with us, saying we ought to go into those places where they have signs outside saying 'Kids eat free!' – and see what happens when we say there's about 20 kids with us! We've never dared to do that – though I think when places have those kinds of promotions, it might just be, say, one child per adult or something like that. So, you think, 'Well, it wouldn't really be worth the hassle anyway.'

Sue: Going out to eat, as long as you're sensible, could be a lot worse – for example, I don't think we've ever been turned away by a restaurant because they didn't like the fact that there were so many of us.

Usually, the only problems we'll find – if we've gone to a big place which we think would be able to cater for us all – is that, after we have said, 'Have you a table for 20?', they have sometimes said, 'Woah! How many? Well, we can't fit you all in at the moment, but if you come back in an hour or so.' Yes, sometimes, they might just say they're sorry, but they can't accommodate such a big number that day, but I don't think anyone has ever told us they have a policy of not accepting such big groups, full stop.

Some restaurants might be surprised at how big the family is, but they don't discriminate against us. As for other places, though, swimming pools can be a nightmare, because they can have an adult to child ratio. If the older ones – the grown-up children – come with us, we will be OK, but we wouldn't be if it was just me and Noel with a load of kids.

Noel: Yeah, it tends to be one adult looking after two children. Another area that smaller families might not think about is the family tickets that are available at a lot of attractions. These are obviously designed to help families save money, but often the deal might just be for two adults and two children, or maybe three children. Sometimes, you'll price it up individually – two adults and all these kids – and that will add up to 'x' amount. Then you'll price it with the family tickets, and it can still be cheaper to buy several family tickets even if you're not taking in the extra adults. You have to be good at maths, too!

Sue: Another thing about being out with the kids is the comments you sometimes get – although I think we get less than we used to years ago, because more people will have seen us on television so they know who we are.

Noel: Years ago, you'd get, 'Blimey, are they all yours?' That was the really common one.

Sue: And, 'Do you not have a telly?' That was another one!

Noel: Also, people would ask, 'Is this a school trip?' And they'd say things like, 'I'm glad I'm not behind you in a queue' or – if they were unlucky – 'Trust me to end up behind you in a queue!' When we moved into the house in Morecambe back in 2004 – which was a former care home – some people thought it had become a children's home!

Sue: We've also had, 'Where are the other mums and dads – it seems to be you two looking after all these children all the time!'

Noel: It's amusing for us, because often you can tell that the person who has made one of these comments thinks they're the first person to have ever said it! And we're just thinking, 'I wish they'd come out with something more original!' We do get some people who have never seen the TV programme, and they'll just be curious – and ask us, 'How do you manage to get around? How do you cope, and keep everyone under control?' That sort of thing. They're just interested, and we're more than happy to chat with them.

Sue: We do get some lovely comments. Like when we go on holiday and we're sitting on the plane, we'll always get the air hostesses saying lovely things like, 'The children have been so fantastic.' Even people who have been on the flight will come up to us when we're waiting for our luggage, and they'll say, 'I just want to say your children are a credit to you – they've been so well-behaved.' They're really nice to hear, those sorts of comments.

Noel: The children are pretty good, I think, in these stressful travelling situations. It can be tedious for everyone. I'd say it's worse for them on busy trains than when they're on a plane, to be honest. On a train, there's no entertainment – there's no TV or anything for them. On a plane, when they're sitting down and they have entertainment in front of them they're just fine. It's the waiting around and having nothing to do when they can get bored – like when they have to be at an airport two or three hours before a flight.

Sue: We've always noticed, or sensed, people staring at us when we're in this big family group of ours – and that can be a bit off-putting. Sometimes you can actually see people counting the number of kids, which is funny! But there are some places where this doesn't happen – because we'd never dream of going to them. For example, although we might choose to eat in a large beer garden, we wouldn't ever walk into a pub itself with a lot of our kids. That is a definite no-no. We also try to avoid areas that are pretty quiet – because we don't want to rock up somewhere with loads of children and spoil it for the few people who are there. We'd just stick out like a sore thumb in those situations.

It's a bit of a balancing act, because you need to find big places – but you want a good number of other people, including other families, to be there. For example, you don't want to walk into a small beer garden where there are just one or two couples trying to have a nice romantic lunch! You don't want to feel uncomfortable – or make other people feel uncomfortable. Ideally, you want to be able to be in a busy place where you can blend in – though not a place which is so busy that there isn't enough room for us all. It can be tricky!

Noel: What smaller families probably take for granted is just being able to turn up somewhere and get a table without any problems at all. They'll probably never be thinking, 'Why wouldn't there be a table for three or four?'

Sue: Whereas we will often have to go in and check to see if there's even a possibility of being able to eat somewhere that afternoon, evening or whatever. The other thing that can be a problem for us is holidays – because we can't always book hotels in the same way other families can. Hotels abroad will usually only cater for family rooms with two adults and a maximum of three children. That's why we tend to book villas, because hotels just wouldn't be suitable for our needs.

Noel: We have stayed in hotels in the past, but it was hard work. The room situation is just so difficult. You might book five rooms, but only use three – because more of the children will end up wanting to be together. It just doesn't really work.

Sue: We've spoken a lot here about what happens when we're out and about with so many kids, and there can be a lot of problems and hassles – but we've never said, 'Oh, we wish our family was smaller' because, for us, the advantages far outweigh the disadvantages. There might be a few things that are difficult for us because of the size of the family, but on the other side of the coin there are so many more occasions when we are just so grateful that we have such a big family because we think it just makes our lives so special. Christmas and birthdays are great examples of that – and going on holidays together, despite the problems there can be at airports.

Noel: And the problems and hassles will never stop us going out and about as a family. So, watch out – the Radfords are coming!

Chapter 25

The next generation: Our brilliant grandchildren

Sue: People might say there's no longer any need for the 'and counting' in the title of the TV programme, because me and Noel won't be having any more kids. But we will hopefully be counting grandchildren for many more years.

Noel: We definitely always wanted grandkids – and hoped to have them. It was always in the back of our minds.

Sue: Yes, definitely. We always thought, 'Oh, we'd love grandkids.' It's been really nice because it means our grandkids have grown up with some of our children as well. They're really good friends, as well as being related to one another. That's just a lovely thing.

Noel: We're so proud of all our grandkids, and we're delighted that they are all so happy and healthy – that's all that matters.

Sue: Exactly!

Daisy Mae
Born to Sophie, August 27, 2012

Noel: Daisy is a very confident young lady.

Sue: She loves dancing and she loves music – and yeah, she's quite sassy!

Noel: We can definitely see some of Sophie, when she was a kid, in Daisy – because Sophie liked to dance and be the centre of attention.

Sue: Yeah, Sophie was also very confident and outgoing.

Ayprill Louise
Born to Sophie, October 13, 2014

Sue: Ayprill is the shyer of the two girls, really. She's very much a mummy's girl, isn't she, Noel?

Noel: Oh yes, definitely. She can be a little bit mischievous but, yeah, she's a lovely little girl.

Sue: Ayprill was born just over three months after our Alfie was stillborn, and when it's Ayprill's birthday you do sometimes think, 'Oh, Alfie would have been the same age – I wonder what he would have been doing today.' But you don't think like that very often, it probably just is on their birthdays.

Leo Thomas
Born to Sophie, December 24, 2015

Noel: It is special that Leo has the same birthday as me! He was very clingy as a kiddie and would never leave his mum's side, but he's not now – he's absolutely fine. He's a lovely lad.

Sue: He and our Archie are very close – they love playing together and spending time together, which is nice.

Noel: And because of Sophie's early work shifts, her three kids will either stay overnight at ours or come first thing in the morning and then join the school run with our kids.

Maisie Paige
Born to Chris, June 3, 2017

Sue: Maisie is quite confident and outgoing, and she loves her gymnastics and is really good at it – a bit like I was when I was younger.

Noel: Yes, Maisie is a very bright and happy little girl – and talented, like Sue!

Jacob Colin
Born to Chris, July 31, 2019

Noel: Jacob just doesn't stop smiling. He is always smiling, isn't he?

Sue: Yeah, he's really happy, and loves playing with his toys – and as Noel says, always smiling and laughing.

Ophelia Jo
Born to Millie, September 10, 2020

Sue: Ophelia is lovely, happy and cheery – she's quite a character, a bit like her mum.

Noel: She can be quite bossy – and she likes to talk! She's another one who's very confident and has the gift of the gab.

Sue: Some of the stuff she comes out with – you can really see Millie in her when Millie was younger.

Oaklyn Nicholas
Born to Chris, September 21, 2021

Sue: He's very shy. But he's only very young, and I'm sure that will change as he gets a little bit older.

Noel: That's what you realise with kids – they do start out one way, and then can very quickly change and develop as they grow.

Sue: And whereas you can see some of Chris when he was younger in Maisie and Jacob, you can't see as much in Oaklyn, I don't think – not yet anyway.

Chester Bleu
Born to Millie, February 20, 2022

Noel: He really started to come into his own after he started walking, and he's another one who is quite a happy little chappie. He's quite content to sit quietly by himself and keep himself busy, happily playing with his toys. He hasn't got a care in the world.

Sue: Yeah, Chester is a lovely little lad – very laid-back and happy.

Mila Eloise
Born to Chloe, July 23, 2022

Sue: Mila is another one who just never stops smiling – she is such a happy little girl. She definitely loves her food – and she's not a fussy eater, either. She'll eat anything – which mums and dads know isn't the case with a lot of very young children.

Noel: Oh, Mila never stops eating! And she loves playing – it's great fun watching her explore and find the joy in things.

Sue: I currently look after Mila on a Monday, and she goes to nursery Tuesday to Friday.

Elodie Jade
Born to Millie, September 19, 2023

Sue: Elodie is a very chilled baby, you don't hear her cry very often. She did have to go into hospital for a few days before she was even two months old, because she was suffering from something called respiratory syncytial virus (RSV), which causes infections of the respiratory tract. But she got through that, made a full recovery and is fine now. Elodie is very smiley and happy - a bit like her sister, Ophelia, when she was a baby. And she looks very much like Ophelia.

Noel: Definitely! And like Sue says, she's very chilled. But the problem me and Sue have in this family, when a new grandchild arrives, is trying to get close enough to get our cuddles – because all the kids want their cuddles, too.

Sue: We're way down the list! You have to try to get in there as quickly as you can.

Chapter 26

The future – it's looking good!

Noel: Because our lives can be so frenetic, we are not the best people for planning ahead – but it is sometimes nice to daydream a little as we wonder how things might be for us in the future.

We currently have 10 grandchildren – at the time of writing! People have asked us how many we think we might end up having – and that's before they go on to mention great grand-children and even, possibly, great, great and, who knows, great, great, great grandchildren!

Sue and I have obviously chatted about it, but it's all so unknowable. It would all be complete guesswork, because you just don't know how your kids' lives will pan out – which ones will want kids and which won't. Some who you think might not have kids might go on to have a few – and vice versa. But yes, you do talk about it – and I think it could be around 40 grandchildren, personally. Though it could end up being many more – maybe 60 or 70, perhaps.

Sue: Yes, we have thought about it – and grandchildren-wise, I think those numbers sound about right. But although it could be 40, or 60, or 70 – or maybe even more – you really just don't know. Some of the kids might not want them, some might only want one or two – it's hard to do anything more than guess, really.

Noel: Millie said she wouldn't be having any – and she recently had her third! It just shows, you never know. It's easier to predict those things about the future we have more control over – like the pie company. As we said earlier, we definitely plan to expand the business. Then, whenever the time is right, the idea would be for other members of the family to take it over.

When I'm ready to retire, I'm hoping some of the kids will already be in the situation where they're basically running it day-to-day – which will make the handover as smooth as possible. I'm 53 now and I'd like it to happen in the next few years if possible – at the age of 55 or 56 would be nice. We'll just have to see.

Sue: I'll be back in the bakery when our youngest, Heidie, goes to school, but, yes, it would be nice for us to be able to take a step back from the business in a few years and let some of the older kids run it.

Noel: At the bakery currently, we've got Chloe, Jack and Luke. I can see Chloe being the main person to take it over – Jack and Luke, I could maybe see them moving onto something else eventually. But you don't know – it might be others who aren't involved at the moment, maybe because they're still at school, who will end up being part of things.

Sue: And the plan for when we're older definitely involves travelling more. We might possibly buy somewhere in Spain – a little holiday home (yes, OK, Noel, not Florida!) While there are plenty of places we'd love to go on holiday, here and abroad. I think whatever happens, we will definitely have a base in this area. As for the kids and where they might end up living, I can see Daniel going further afield – he was talking about going to Australia at some point, so I can see him possibly moving away. But the likes of Jack and Luke and the rest of them, I can't really see that.

Noel: No, not for the next few years anyway. I think Luke might eventually move away, if he changes his career or gets a partner – and as for the younger ones, we'll just have to wait and see. But yes, I feel Daniel for sure could end up moving away – I could see Chloe and her family moving away at some point, too. But I think the pull of a big family is quite strong, and it might be that even the ones who do end up moving away might only do so for a limited time before returning. But again, you just don't know how things will work out.

Sue: It will be interesting to see how all their lives develop and where they all end up. But I think we know where we will end up – although there will hopefully be a lot of travelling, we will be staying in this area and going from looking after a lot of kids to helping to look after a lot of grandkids! But that would be fine by us – and we do help an awful lot at the moment, anyway. We're very hands-on with them, which we love, and I think that will continue – we just can't see that changing.

Noel: Regarding what me and Sue want to end up doing together, it's going away on holiday that we love. Going to the Maldives for our 30th wedding anniversary in 2022 really gave us the bug to do a lot more travelling together like that – it was so nice just to be able to spend time with each other.

Sue: I'd love to go to Bora Bora, and the Seychelles – and I'd love to go back to the Maldives because that was just incredible, and go back to Australia, too.

Noel: There are some city breaks we'd like to have, like New York and Singapore. And on a personal note, I'd like to get my pilot's licence – but I only took my first lesson a few months ago.

Sue: As well as expanding the bakery business, we also hope the Radford Family media business – the filming for Channel 5, our YouTube channel and so on – will continue. There are always new stories, always things happening in the family – the kids getting older and their lives developing, more grandkids coming along and so on. I hope it all continues, and I think it will.

Noel: We also hope it will open doors for the kids, as well, so they can maybe start their own media things if they want to. The thing is, social media is changing and developing all the time – YouTube, for example, isn't as lucrative as it used to be. We've just got to do our best to keep up with the trends.

And who knows, there may be more books, as well!

That's the future sorted out, then – though we reserve the right to end up doing everything very differently. We are Radfords, after all – things don't always go according to plan!

Sue: The readers have probably noticed that already, Noel! What was that we said all those years ago about us having just three children?

Noel: I know, but if you're enjoying doing something then why stop?

Sue: We really hope you've enjoyed finding out more about our ongoing adventure. We've certainly had a lot of fun putting this book together.

Noel: Looking back on our lives has been really special, and I've remembered things I'd totally forgotten.

Oh, one last thing, Sue, do you think we should ask if anyone fancies volunteering for a spot of babysitting?

Sue: What's he like?

Thanks so much for reading!

What the kids say about Mum and Dad

Noel

Right, Sue, it's time for us to take a back
seat – for some reason we agreed that
the kids should be given their say, too!
Maybe I should have bribed them first.
But they'll say some nice things about
us, won't they? WON'T THEY?

Sue

There's only one way to find out.
Here they all are, in order of age...

Chris

Mum is a genuine parent; helpful and caring. She cares for all the kids, and will help us all in any way she can if we are ever struggling. Mum's also a good laugh – there's never a dull day. Mum and Dad are both calm people – you would think, after having 22 kids, they'd have no hair left!

Being part of a big family is all I've ever known. I think I might find it odd being in a family of just two or three children. All the kids are hard-working – mum and dad brought us up to be like that. Dad works hard at the bakery, then comes home to help mum with the kids – they both do so much for everyone. It's non-stop for them from the moment they get up – they probably get just one hour to themselves during the day.

Christmas is always the best time of year to be a part of this family, just because everyone gets together. A few of us have moved out over the years, but Christmas is one of those times when everyone is together – including the kids and the grandkids.

Sophie

Mum is an incredible woman – she's quite inspirational, because not many people can say they've had 22 children! She's a great role model, and such a lovely and down-to-earth woman. And I love my dad, he is absolutely brilliant – one of a kind! He has the best sense of humour, and will do anything for anyone. His work ethic has completely rubbed off on all of us.

Mum and Dad brought us all up to appreciate the value of

money and hard work. When I was younger, growing up here wasn't so crazy because there was only me and a few others – though as the years went by it got a bit crazier, but I wouldn't have wanted it any other way.

You're never lonely in this family – I love it. Christmas is always really special. It's just great when the house is so busy although I don't know how mum and dad also cope with seven dogs!

Chloe

Mum and Dad are so laid-back. They're like friends, as well as being parents. They're not strict, and it's a really nice home environment. I really enjoyed growing up in the family. I never ever wished I was an only child or part of a smaller family. But I feel like you've got to be a certain kind of person to have that many kids, because if you were kind of easily-stressed then you would just lose it completely.

I've got one child, and since I've had Mila I look at Mum and Dad and think, 'How have you actually done it?'

Jack

Mum and Dad are very caring and loving parents. They've always been there for me. You can read nonsense online about how, because they have so many children, they don't have time for all their kids – but it's not like that at all. Whenever any one of us needs them, they are always there.

They're the best parents anyone could ask for. Growing up in such a big family is all I know. To me it's just been normal – it's loud and always busy, but that's just normal for me.

Daniel

Mum is a very caring and loving woman. She couldn't try any harder for us. I couldn't have any more respect for her. She always thinks about herself last – because she's making sure everyone else in the family is happy. Dad is very similar to my mum – he's very hard-working and dedicated, which sets a good example for all of his children.

All those who have left school and college have gone straight into work, but it starts before then. When I was 14 or 15, I was helping out my dad on my days off and Saturdays, because seeing him work so hard made me want to work hard. We all take pride in the family business and I think everyone who is old enough has been involved in the bakery at some time or other.

And also like Mum, Dad's a very loving person – he's always there if you need to have a chat about literally anything. I couldn't imagine being in a smaller family.

I'm working away from home at the moment, living with one of my mates – and I'm coming home from work and it's just complete silence. It is nice, but it just seems weird when there's no noise. Back home, I think Christmas is the best time of year to be part of the family. The whole family – including Mum's side and Dad's side – get together and it's just great.

Luke

Mum and Dad… they're just not natural! They are way too laid-back! You look at how many kids they have and what it's like in the house, and you'd think, 'This would stress anybody out' but they just crack on. They've got seven dogs, as well! But growing up in the family has been really fun, I've really enjoyed it.

There are days when you think it's just too loud, when there's constant noise, with all the smaller kids – and the dogs – running around. But the positives far outweigh any negatives.

Millie

My mum – I could not do what she does on a daily basis; all the washing is endless, the house cleaning is endless, the shopping and generally running the house. And yet she's very, very laid-back. Dad is definitely a laid-back person – even more than my mum. I just think he lets whatever mum says go! He's always cracking jokes – and it's always dad jokes!

My friends always ask me about what it was like growing up in this family, but to all us siblings it's just been normal. There's always company – there's always someone here.

Katie

I love my mum. She's very calm and just gets on with it. She never seems to get stressed out, which is a miracle. It makes me think that yes, I'd like to have kids – but just not as many as my mum and dad! Dad is a funny one – he's a character. When my mates first come round here, they say, 'It's so loud' – but then they'll come round again and say, 'There doesn't seem like there's so many of you in the house'. They never believe me at first when I say there are 22 of us.

James

My mum is a beautiful woman. She does everything for the family. She's always very busy looking after us all, and she treats us all equally. Dad is a very hard-working man. He's brought us all up in the right way, to respect work – and to respect each other. I think it's always been a good thing to be part of such a big family, because you're never lonely – you've always got someone to talk to and you're never bored. I absolutely love it.

Ellie

My mum is the best! She's like a best friend – I can tell her anything. My dad's the same and he's very funny – I think I get my silliness from him.

Growing up with so many siblings has been normal to me, but when I go to my friends' houses and they've only got one or two siblings, it's like, 'Where's all the noise? It's so quiet here!' Then when people come to my house, it's all, 'It's so noisy, Ellie!' But I'm used to it, so it doesn't bother me.

Holidays are very fun with my family, too. You're never left out when you're going on a ride because you're always with other siblings – family holidays are just top tier!

Aimee

Mum and Dad are inseparable. They're lovely parents and mean the world to me – family is everything. There's always a lot of fun in our house.

Christmas is my favourite time because the whole family is together – somehow, we all manage to fit in the kitchen and dining room. It's definitely quieter at my friends' houses – and sometimes I think it's a bit too quiet for me and I have to come back home, back to the noise!

Josh

Mum is a really nice woman – she's really caring. But even though she does so much, she's very chilled out. She's also a really good friend. My dad is so funny, and he's also so caring – he does so much stuff for us, too. He's a great cook, too – every meal here is just so good. And you're never really bored in this house, because there are so many brothers and sisters.

Max

Mum is very energetic – she likes to do a lot. When we go on holiday, a lot of the days will be really planned out by her. She's very organised. Dad is very hard-working as well – when he does something, he does it 100%. And on holiday and days out, he's been on every ride I know of.

It's normal for me to have all these brothers and sisters, but it is very chaotic. Some days you can't find a single place anywhere in the house where it's quiet. But there's a lot of fun.

Tillie

I think my mum is a very kind, passionate and thoughtful woman. And my dad likes to achieve things – he's very determined and ambitious. He's also very kind. The best thing about living here is that whenever I'm bored and there is nothing to do, I have my siblings to hang around and have a laugh with.

Oscar

Mum and Dad like to take us out to places and on holidays; they like to treat us. They also work very hard around the house and we have a lot of fun together in the house. And on holiday, we go to lots of fun places – go on rollercoasters and things like that. I like going away in the motorhome, too.

Casper

Mum and Dad really care about us. They are always really busy and they're really hard-working around the house. They are also resilient. It's really good having so many brothers and sisters. Oscar is who I'm closest to – we're very close in age.

Hallie

My mum is a good mum and she is kind and nice to me. She always looks after me. I like it when we go on holiday. My dad makes nice meals and I most like to eat his pies! It's great having all my brothers and sisters.

Phoebe

My mummy is a good mummy. She wears nice dresses and clothes. And she's a kind mummy. Daddy is funny and he is a good cook. I love having lots of brothers and sisters, and they all look after me and play with me.

Archie

I think my mum and dad are great. I like my mum because she gives me sweets and is kind to me. My dad makes good pies! He's a very good cook. I also love having lots of brothers and sisters – and I love playing in the garden.

Bonnie

My mummy gives me lots of hugs, that's what I like best of all. Daddy gives me a lot of hugs as well as mummy. I like his cooking – he makes me pies and Thai noodles. They're great. I love playing with Hallie and all my brothers and sisters.

Heidie

I like dancing with my mummy and daddy! They hug me and I like that. And I love Christmas. I like playing with everyone – and I like playing with (my niece) Ophelia. I have lots of fun.

Noel: Ah, I'm welling up here, Sue – that was lovely, wasn't it?

Sue: I think we did OK, didn't we? Are you sure you didn't bribe them? What lovely children they all are!

The Radford
Family Timeline

Noel

We realise there's a lot to keep track
of with our family, and things can seem
complicated, which is why I think the
following dates, facts and figures will
be helpful – not least for me, so I don't
miss the kids' birthdays! But seriously,
we have packed quite a lot in over
the years – and hopefully there is still
much more to come!

December 24, 1970

Noel is born in Stockport, Greater Manchester.

He is adopted by David and Val Radford, from Manchester, when he is 10 days old. After living in different parts of the country – including Bollington in Cheshire, Evesham in Worcestershire and Lowther and then Morland in Cumbria – Noel's family puts down roots in Kendal, Cumbria, when he is seven. Noel learns he is adopted when he is seven or eight.

March 22, 1975

Sue – short for Suzanne – is born in Bishop Auckland, County Durham. She is adopted by Christine and Colin Baines from Kendal when she is a few days old. Like Noel, she learns she is adopted when she is seven or eight.

1978 – 1982

After his family settles in Kendal, Noel attends Castle Park Primary School.

1979 – 1986

Sue attends Heron Hill Primary School in Kendal.

1982

Noel and Sue, whose families live in cul-de-sacs separated by an alleyway, meet for the first time – he is 11 and she is seven. Noel initially becomes friends with Sue's older brother, Stephen.

1982 – 1987

Noel attends Kirkbie Kendal Secondary School in Kendal.

1986 – 1991

Sue attends Kirkbie Kendal Secondary School in Kendal.

August 4, 1988

Noel and Sue start going out together.

September/October 1988

Sue discovers she is pregnant. Noel leaves college so he can start earning money, as a trainee baker at the Gateway supermarket in Kendal.

May 7, 1989

Noel and Sue's first child, Christopher, known as Chris, is born.

Initially, Chris lives with Sue at her parents' home. Sue's mum helps look after Chris during the day, enabling Sue to carry on attending school until she is 16.

Noel is living at home when Chris is born, but soon gets a flat.

Sue and Chris spend time visiting Noel in the flat, before returning to Sue's parents' home at night.

August 1991

Noel, now 20, Sue, now 16, and Chris move into their first home, a rented council house in Kendal.

September 26, 1992

Noel, now 21, and Sue, now 17, marry at Kendal Parish Church.

January 1993

Noel, Sue and Chris move to another rented council house, also in Kendal.

December 13, 1993

Noel and Sue's second child Sophie Rose is born.

May 1995

Noel, Sue, Chris and Sophie move to another council house, also in Kendal, which they later buy.

July 31, 1995

Third child Chloe Anne is born.

April 9, 1997

Fourth child Jack Richard is born.

February 12, 1999

Sue and Noel open a pie shop and bakery in Heysham, near Morecambe. They keep its longstanding name – Faraday's – for many years.

By this time, following his first job in the Gateway supermarket, Noel has also gathered experience working at Rigg's bakery, in Kendal; the Morrisons supermarket in-store bakery in Kendal, and the Hazelmere bakery in Grange-over-Sands.

March 3, 1999

Fifth child Daniel Leon is born.

October 1, 2000
Sixth child Luke James is born.

December 2000
The ever-growing family move to a bigger house, in Heysham. Just before Christmas, Noel and Sue make "the worst decision of our lives" – taking a huge loan to lease a second shop, this one in Kendal.

February – September 2001
Foot-and-mouth disease kills tourism in the Lake District and the whole of Cumbria, and the couple's dream becomes a debt-ridden nightmare.

August 29, 2001
Seventh child Millie Jo is born.

September 2001
Noel and Sue cut their losses and shut up shop in Kendal.

August 2002
The family move to a four-bedroom house in Heysham, which they extend to five bedrooms.

November 14, 2002
Eighth child Katie Louise is born.

June 2003
Noel has a vasectomy, immediately regrets it and decides to have a reversal. The couple begin saving up.

October 17, 2003
Ninth child James Edward is born.

June 2004
Noel undergoes his vasectomy reversal.

August 2004
The Radfords move into a former care home in Morecambe, which has 10 bedrooms.

May 6, 2005
Tenth child Ellie May is born.

April 21, 2006
Eleventh child Aimee Elizabeth is born.

July 3, 2007
Twelfth child Josh Benjamin is born.

December 11, 2008
Thirteenth child Max Joseph is born.

May 2, 2010
Fourteenth child Tillie May is born.

October 22, 2011
Fifteenth child Oscar Will is born.

January 17, 2012
The Radfords appear on TV for the first time, on the Channel 4 documentary series *15 Kids and Counting*.

August 27, 2012
Noel and Sue's first grandchild, Daisy Mae, is born to their second child, Sophie.

October 3, 2012
Sixteenth child Casper Theo is born.

July 6, 2014
Seventeenth child Alfie Thomas is stillborn.

October 13, 2014
Second grandchild, Ayprill Louise, is born to Sophie.

June 3, 2015
Eighteenth child Hallie Alphia Beau is born.

November 2015
The Radford Pie Company is launched online.

December 24, 2014
Third grandchild, Leo Thomas, is born to Sophie.

July 24, 2016
Nineteenth child Phoebe Willow is born.

June 3, 2017
Fourth grandchild, Maisie Paige, is born to first child Chris.

September 18, 2017
Twentieth child Archie Rowan is born.

September 26, 2017
Noel and Sue celebrate their silver wedding anniversary.

November 6, 2018
Twenty-first child Bonnie Raye is born.

July 31, 2019
Fifth grandchild, Jacob Colin, is born to Chris.

April 3, 2020
Twenty-second child Heidie Rose is born.

September 10, 2020
Sixth grandchild, Ophelia Jo, is born to seventh child Millie.

February 22, 2021
Britain's Biggest Family: 22 Kids and Counting debuts on Channel 5.

September 21, 2021
Seventh grandchild, Oaklyn Nicholas, is born to Chris.

September 27, 2021
The family business opens a bigger bakehouse, in an industrial unit less than two miles from the shop. The bakehouse was previously attached to the shop.

February 20, 2022
Eighth grandchild, Chester Bleu, is born to Millie.

July 23, 2022
Ninth grandchild, Mila Eloise, is born to third child Chloe.

September 26, 2022
Noel and Sue celebrate their 30th wedding anniversary.

November 2022
The couple's shop, Faraday's, is renamed the Radford Pie Company.

September 19, 2023
Tenth grandchild, Elodie Jade, is born to Millie.

February 12, 2024
Sue and Noel celebrate 25 years of the family business.

February 29, 2024
This book is published!

Acknowledgements

Sue: The first people we would like to thank are our children. I can't imagine life without our kids. I feel so thankful and so lucky to have them.

Noel: They make us happy every day of our lives. Thanks kids – we're so proud of you all.

Sue: And thank you to our grandchildren, for also bringing us so much love and joy. Again, we feel so lucky and blessed to have them in our lives.

Noel: When you look at your grandchildren you start to look at things through their eyes, and think back to how you used to look at your grandparents – there is also that same sort of bond.

Sue: I want to thank my mum and my late dad – for their love, their support and for giving me such a great life. And thanks to Stephen, for being the best big brother anyone could wish for. We were so lucky to be adopted by our mum and dad.

Noel: And I want to thank my dad and my late mum – they always showed me enormous love, and were there when I needed them most at the very start of my journey as a dad. I am so glad I was adopted by them. Thanks, too, to my brilliant big brother, Ian, who has always been there for me.

Sue: Me and Noel both want to thank all those friends who stood by us when, as teenagers, we were expecting our first child, Chris. Thank you, especially, to my lifelong friends Lorraine, Julie and Karen. Their support has never been forgotten by us, and it never will be.

Noel: At that difficult point in our lives, we were so lucky to have such great parents and brothers – while the friends who stuck by us were also priceless. We thank them all from the bottom of our hearts. I also want to thank Mr Lawson, my old tutor at Kendal College – where I was training to be a chef, doing my City and Guilds 706/1 qualification in catering, when Sue told me she was expecting our first baby. I needed to leave college and start earning, and it was Mr Lawson who made the phone call to the Gateway supermarket – which also put us on the road to being able to open our own bakery business. I also owe a lot to the late Jim Reed – who was another tutor at the college, although he didn't teach me. Each student had to do a work placement, and Mr Reed obviously saw something in my college application because he picked me out to work in the hotel he owned. I had wanted to work as a chef for years, and I have him to thank for making it happen.

Sue: My eternal thanks to all of the midwives who helped bring our children into the world. We owe you so much!

Noel: And our everlasting gratitude also goes to the late Dr Richard Wilson, who carried out my vasectomy reversal at the time when we had only nine children. He gave us so many great gifts by carrying out that one procedure.

Sue: A special thank you to Celia Sykes, the bereavement midwife at the Royal Lancaster Infirmary when we lost Alfie. She was just incredible and I don't think I would have had the strength to carry on and have more children without her support.

Noel: Thank you to Kathryn and Robert Caunce, and everyone at Ascension and Cliff Small Independent Family Funeral Directors, who were so good to us after Alfie died – even after his funeral had taken place. They suggested Hale Carr Cemetery for Alfie's final resting place, and we were so grateful to them for that because it was the perfect spot.

Sue: They were brilliant. When our next child, Hallie, was born, Kathryn came out to see us – she was lovely.

Noel: And Robert, a Preston North End supporter, got me and a couple of our lads tickets when Preston played our family's team, Liverpool. That was such a kind gesture.

Sue: They are such kind and thoughtful people. Our special thanks also go to all the fantastic doctors and medical staff at the Royal Lancaster Infirmary who helped save Tillie's life when she was so poorly. We have also enjoyed a great relationship with Leroy James, the orthopaedic surgeon at Alder Hey Children's Hospital in Liverpool, who has performed miracles for Tillie. As well as being a brilliant surgeon, he is also such a lovely and funny man – whenever Tillie was feeling down, he would come in all bubbly and cheerful and lift her spirits.

Noel: He's such a down-to-earth guy and we all just love him.

Sue: And we'll be forever grateful to him for everything he has done for Tillie.

Noel: Thanks to the Morecambe newspaper *The Visitor* –

including former reporter and content editor Greg Lambert – for publishing the very first story on our family, back in 2008. This was the start of so much – it eventually led to us appearing on television, and launching our own social media empire.

Sue: Thank you to everyone involved in making the programmes for Channel 4 and Channel 5. It was Channel 4 who started the ball rolling by giving us a chance to first appear on TV, and Channel 5 has been brilliant in taking everything further. Their programmes on our family just seem to get better – and more popular – with each series. And our thanks, also, to all the viewers who take the time to watch us – and especially those who have sent us so many kind and lovely messages over the years.

Noel: Thanks also to the inventors of YouTube, Instagram, Facebook and TikTok – and, of course, our thanks go to everyone who has bought a Radford's pie!

Sue: And there are so many people who work in the tourism and hospitality industry who deserve our thanks and praise for showing great patience and kindness when serving us and our children. Thank you for keeping a smile on your faces, even in the most stressful of situations!

Noel: And again – but this time from me – thanks to you for reading this book. We really do hope you have enjoyed it.

* * *

And finally...

Sue: I want to say the most special of thank yous to Noel – for being the most amazing husband, as well as the most amazing dad to our children.

We're just so very thankful to have you, love!

Noel: And my most special thank you goes to Sue, who has always been the most brilliant wife and mum. Me and all the kids are so thankful to her for everything she does for the family.

You do everything for us, Sue – and we love you for it!